CASSELL CARAVEL BOOKS

A CASSELL CARAVEL BOOK

BEETHOVEN

By the Editors of
HORIZON MAGAZINE

Author
DAVID JACOBS

Consultant
ELLIOT FORBES

Professor of Music, Harvard University

Cassell · London

© 1970 by American Heritage Publishing Co., Inc., 551 Fifth Avenue, New York, New
York 10017. All rights reserved under Berne and Pan-American Copyright Conventions.
Trademark CARAVEL registered United States Patent Office
First published in Great Britain 1970
I.S.B.N. 0 304 93658 8

FOREWORD

Ludwig van Beethoven, the son and grandson of musicians, was born in Bonn, Germany, just two hundred years ago. During his lifetime his music became known all over Europe, and after his death his fame as a composer spread around the world. His contemporaries were immediately pleased by his early pieces, which were so reminiscent of those written by his illustrious predecessors Mozart and Haydn. The Romantics of the nineteenth century found their inspiration in the compositions of Beethoven's middle years, while today the difficult, brooding works of his late years are most admired by serious listeners.

It is appropriate that the story of the composer's life be told again on the bicentenary of his birth. Recent research has clarified many of the obscure points in that tormented life, and the complex, often paradoxical personality that emerges provides a striking contrast to the powerful serenity of the music.

The short, swarthy boy became a strong, mercurial man. He loved many women but never married; depending upon his mood, he treated his friends and family with great warmth or with cutting vindictiveness. Growing increasingly deaf, he became sullen and bitter. Still, despite his moodiness, his slovenliness, and his outspoken republicanism, he was an honored guest in all the great houses of autocratic Vienna.

During Beethoven's lifetime Europe was swept by change. The right of kings to rule was challenged first in thought and then in deed by the French Revolution. The liberals who rallied to that cause subsequently supported Napoleon when he and his armies swept across western Europe, ostensibly bringing with them the ideals of democracy. Then, when Napoleon crowned himself emperor, Beethoven was as profoundly disillusioned as the other liberals of the age. Paradoxically, the antidemocratic reaction had begun in Austria even before Napoleon's coronation. The reforms of the Austrian emperor Joseph II were revoked by his successors, and Beethoven, the revolutionary, spent the better part of his life in one of Europe's most reactionary countries.

This account of Beethoven's life is cast against the panorama of the times in which he lived: both perspectives are documented by paintings and drawings by artists who were Beethoven's contemporaries. The resultant portrait of a man and an age adds another dimension to music that has become part of our heritage.

THE EDITORS

Memorabilia of Beethoven's life are set out on the dead composer's desk: his glasses, an ear trumpet, a bust of Brutus, a miniature of a favorite lady pianist, paperweights given him by a princely patron, and a handwritten plea to the courts asking for custody of his beloved nephew, Karl.

RIGHT: *This lithograph of the composer in a characteristic pose but with an oddly wistful expression was copied from a drawing that depicted him in 1826, only a year before he died.*

BEETHOVEN-HAUS, BONN

COVER: *Beethoven was most delighted by the treatment of his hair in this 1818 drawing by August von Klöber. He remarked that other portraits had made him look too well groomed.*

BEETHOVEN-HAUS, BONN

ENDSHEETS: *Beethoven did not compose easily, as this manuscript page from his* Missa Solemnis *testifies. He worked on the mass intermittently for about three and a half years.*

NEW YORK PUBLIC LIBRARY

TITLE PAGE: *When the London firm of John Broadwood sent Beethoven this piano as a present, he was so delighted that he would not take a colleague's advice and have it tuned.*

CONTENTS

I

THE BEETHOVENS OF BONN

"... what a humiliation," Beethoven wrote, "when one stood beside me and heard a flute in the distance and *I heard nothing*, or someone heard *the shepherd singing* and again I heard nothing. . . ."

The composer was recalling a country walk he had taken in 1802 near Heiligenstadt, Austria. His hearing had been failing for several years, and on his doctor's advice he was spending the summer at the quiet little village not far from Vienna.

During his first days in Heiligenstadt, Beethoven had great hopes for recovery. But by the end of the summer, he realized that his affliction had grown worse. At thirty-two he was a brilliant performer and a promising composer. And at thirty-two he was being forced to accept the bleak prospect of a future without his "noblest faculty, my hearing."

He almost despaired. ". . . if I approach near to people," he wrote, "a hot terror seizes upon me, a fear that I may be subjected to the danger of letting my condition be observed. . . ." Perhaps considering suicide, he wrote a will. He later admitted: ". . . I would have put an end to my life—only art it was that withheld me, ah it seemed impossible to leave the world until I had produced all that I felt called upon to produce. . . ."

In the fall Beethoven returned to Vienna; in the months that followed, his depression began to disappear. It did not so much lift as it was thrust aside by the will of the composer.

"I will take fate by the throat;" he had written to a friend, "it shall not wholly overcome me. Oh, it is so beautiful to live—to live a thousand times! I feel that I am not made for a quiet life."

Within four years of the gloomy Heiligenstadt summer,

An engraving made in 1790, twenty years after Ludwig van Beethoven was born there, shows the German city of Bonn to be hardly a city at all, but more of an elegant, quiet village port on the unspoiled banks of the Rhine.

The Beethoven family lived in an upstairs apartment at Number 934 Rheingasse in Bonn (shown here in a contemporary painting) during a good part of the composer's youth.

he was being called master—a worthy successor to the great Mozart himself, Vienna's earlier adopted son.

Mozart was already a prolific composer and a renowned child prodigy of fourteen when Ludwig van Beethoven was born in the German town of Bonn on December 16, 1770. The son of a poor musician, Beethoven spent the greater part of his youth with his parents and his two brothers in an upstairs apartment in the Rheingasse, a street in a well-kept working-class neighborhood.

Much of what is known of Beethoven's youth comes from the recollections of the landlord's son, Gottfried Fischer. Ten years younger than Ludwig, Gottfried wrote his memoirs when he was sixty: what he says is interesting but not always accurate. However, Gottfried's description of Beethoven as a boy is borne out by others. Ludwig was short for his age, but built compactly and sturdily. His head, resting on a thick neck, was somewhat too large in proportion to his body. His angular forehead and jaw were prominent, his eyes small, dark, and bright, his nose broad and rounded at the end. His complexion was swarthy —strikingly so in a country of fair-skinned people. Indeed, because of his dark coloring, the Fischers called him *der Spagnol*, "the Spaniard."

He was in fact not Spanish, but of German and Flemish descent. Originally his father's family came from Flanders. The Spaniard's paternal grandmother, however, was German, as was his mother.

Some time before the end of the seventeenth century the Beethoven family moved to the Flemish town of Mechlin, where Ludwig's great-grandfather was a baker and a part-time dealer in Dutch paintings and lace from Brussels. His son Louis was born in 1712.

Louis was a choirboy in a Mechlin church, and his exquisite singing voice attracted the attention of local clergy and musicians, who encouraged his parents to give him a musical education. While still a boy, Louis became court organist in the town of Louvain, fifteen miles away. At the age of eighteen he went to Bonn to become a singer in the court chapel. There he remained, steadily rising in his profession and in the eyes of his patrons, becoming a respected member of the German community. Soon even he stopped thinking of himself by his Franco-Flemish name, Louis, and called himself Ludwig, as his neighbors did.

Bonn was a clean, comfortable hamlet on the Rhine, a dreamy, almost timeless place with no more than ten thousand inhabitants. Built in the Middle Ages, Bonn in many

J. G. WALTHER, *Musikalisches Lexicon*, LEIPZIG, 1732

The composer's grandfather Louis made his name in musical circles by singing in church, accompanied by orchestras not very different from the one shown here.

During the eighteenth century the Market Square in Bonn was a tranquil spot for an afternoon stroll. The imposing building at the far end of the square is the City Hall.

ways had retained much of its medieval character. Its architecture was old-fashioned, the pace of life unhurried. There were no factories, little commerce, no suggestion of the increasingly industrial society that Europe was becoming. In the medieval tradition, one man was both political ruler and religious leader. The diocese of Cologne was also the province, or Electorate, of Cologne; the archbishop of the diocese was also the ruler, or Prince Elector, of the re-

gion. Bonn, sixteen miles from Cologne, was the seat of the
Electoral Court; indeed, that was its only reason for being.
As an eighteenth-century visitor noted, accurately, "All
of Bonn is fed from the Prince's kitchen."

In a subtler way, however, Bonn was a typical European
capital of the late 1700's. At that time thoughts of revolution
were stirring on the Continent; subjects began to feel that
their rulers' excesses and abuses were not necessarily part

15

of the Divine Order and need not be tolerated blindly. Some monarchs responded by becoming more rigid and more oppressive, while others attempted to deal with the unrest by being, or appearing to be, more tolerant toward new attitudes. Some even affected an interest and belief in the enlightened ideas of such writers as Voltaire and Rousseau, whose works, while advocating the extension of personal and political freedom, were nonetheless very popular in many European palaces. These more liberal rulers may not have created democratic institutions, but they did, up to a point, allow and even encourage their subjects to think the new democratic thoughts.

Germany and Austria were fragmented into principalities of various sizes and strengths that were ruled by Hapsburg, Hohenzollern, and Hanover princes. These three ancient dynasties produced a fair share of treacherous and despotic men, but also a remarkable number of sincerely—if often superficially—liberal leaders. One way in which they demonstrated their liberalism was not only by patronizing the arts—which, after all, royalty had been doing for centuries—but also by making the arts available to all their subjects.

Despite its smallness, Bonn was the seat of an Electoral Court. As such it was a cultural center on a scale that made it comparable to a modern city with a hundred times its population. Plays in French, German, Italian, and Spanish were offered regularly; operas and comic operas from Rome and Vienna were given public performances as quickly as they could be imported. Almost every stage presentation was preceded or followed by a concert of serious music.

In Bonn music was the chief love of the Electoral Court. The Prince Elector dined to chamber music, conversed to chamber music, received dignitaries to chamber music, performed chamber music, knew his country's folk songs, and danced. Prince Elector Clemens August, for whom Louis van Beethoven worked during much of his tenure in Bonn, was said to have died from too much dancing. Perhaps the Court believed that the music that filled the air of Bonn would soothe the revolutionary spirit. Music could not do that, of course, but it did create an atmosphere of gaiety, which made it difficult for people to proceed from revolutionary thought to revolutionary action.

Materially, Bonn was good to Louis van Beethoven, the grandfather of the famous composer. When Prince Elector Clemens August died in 1761, his successor, Max Friedrich, elevated Beethoven to the position of *Kapellmeis-*

This portrait of Louis van Beethoven probably was painted after he became Kapellmeister, *or chief musician, to the Prince Elector at Bonn.*

ter—essentially, chief musician to the court. Most holders of that highly respected position were composers, but Beethoven was not. That he was promoted anyway suggests that his musical ability and his skill at handling musicians must have been extraordinary. His salary from the court probably assured the family a comfortable existence, but Beethoven supplemented his income in a small way by exporting the sweet Rhineland wines to the Low Countries.

The *Kapellmeister* profited little from his earnings, however. His wife, Maria, was excessively fond of the wine so easily accessible to her and became an alcoholic. Her drinking cost her husband dearly in reputation and fortune, and eventually he had to commit her to an asylum. Unfortunately, their son Johann later developed the same weakness.

"Johann the Walker" his father had called him. Taller and better looking than *Kapellmeister* Beethoven, Johann also was quieter, less ambitious, and less talented. But he loved nature and enjoyed walking for hours along the banks of the Rhine and in the woods outside Bonn. Moreover, he was a competent musician, employed by the Prince Elector to sing in the chapel and teach violin and clavier. He apparently had a streak of independence in him, because in 1767 he married—against his father's wishes—Magdalena Kewerich, the daughter of a cook. Louis considered

Johann and Magdalena van Beethoven, the composer's parents, are depicted in posthumous engravings. No contemporary portraits of the two elder Beethovens have survived.

her beneath his son's station, although in fact Magdalena's maternal ancestors were respectable and prosperous.

In the early years the marriage of Johann and Magdalena van Beethoven was a happy one. They were poor, but Johann was at least steadily employed; and each monthly payday he dutifully handed over his wages to his wife, a more thrifty type than he. A very serious woman— according to an acquaintance, no one ever saw her smile— Magdalena was much admired by her neighbors for her kindheartedness, prudence, and competence. Indeed, Frau Beethoven's goodness ultimately overcame her father-in-law's hostility, and before long the aging gentleman was a frequent caller at her tiny, spotlessly clean home.

As music was more than a mere pastime in Bonn, so, too, it was more than a profession to the young Beethovens. Music and talk of music filled their home and their lives. Through music Johann even communicated his affection for Magdalena. On Magdalena's Day—the religious feast day honoring the saint for whom Frau Beethoven was named—Johann would honor his wife with a musical evening. An observer one year described the ceremony: The night before, the housewife was sent to bed early. Borrowed music stands then were brought from the church in absolute silence and put in place in the living room, right where Grandfather Louis's portrait hung. A sort of canopy was arranged with flowers, laurel, and foliage. As soon as all was ready, the tuning-up began; this woke the mother, who soon appeared, charmingly dressed, and was led to the chair adorned for her under the canopy. Then the glorious music began. All the sleeping neighborhood awoke and listened. Musicians, actors, and friends of the family feasted and danced until an early hour.

There were such moments always, but only moments: happiness was not the rule in the Beethoven household. In a rare display of candor, Magdalena herself summed up her life when she said, "What is marriage? At first a little joy, then a chain of sorrows."

She had seven children in all, but only three survived infancy. Poverty always was threatening, particularly after the death of old Louis in 1773: the *Kapellmeister* apparently had had an intimidating, though stabilizing, effect on his son. As Johann began to drink more, he brought home less and less of his pay, and his wife had to make ends meet on a pitifully small budget. Fortunately, he was not a vicious or violent drunkard. But a drunkard he was and a constant source of worry to his wife and three sons. Gottfried Fischer

Mozart was not a violinist by inclination, but he kept in practice to please his father. This is the instrument he used as a child.

recalled that when the Beethoven boys learned that their father was drunk, "all three were straightaway on the spot, worried, and tried in the most winning way to induce their papa to go quietly home with them, so as not to make a scene; they would say soothingly, 'O Papächen, Papächen!' and then he would comply. He was not quarrelsome in his cups, but merry and lively, so we in the house would hardly notice anything."

Johann van Beethoven was more ambitious for his sons than for himself. He discovered what he thought was a model father in another musician, Leopold Mozart of Salzburg. A first-rate player and composer working for the Hapsburgs of Austria, Leopold Mozart had two very talented children: a girl, Maria Anna, and a boy, Wolfgang. Their father introduced them to the German and Austrian courts when the girl was eleven and her brother six. Although both children were musical prodigies, Wolfgang in particular captivated his royal patrons. By the age of eight he was a respected virtuoso; at eleven he was an important composer; and in 1770, when he was fourteen, he was already among the Continent's major musical figures.

In 1770, then, young Wolfgang Amadeus Mozart was the envy of many European parents. Johann van Beethoven was particularly aware of him because in that year his own son was born and named Ludwig, after the *Kapellmeister*.*

---

*Another son had been born to the Beethovens a year before. Also named Ludwig, the infant had died at the age of six days.

It was this Ludwig who would be called *der Spagnol* by his neighbors. But however distinguished his future, this Ludwig van Beethoven simply was not cut out to be another Wolfgang Amadeus Mozart.

Mozart was a brilliant, graceful, delicate, and beautiful boy—a genius, to be sure, but one who won the affection of the courts of Europe with his childlike and always proper manners and his personal bearing. Ludwig was unpretty, clumsy, unkempt, and unsociable. Mozart loved music and accepted without question the discipline necessary to nurture his talent. Ludwig probably never stopped to consider

At seven the child prodigy Wolfgang Amadeus Mozart had to sit on a cushion in order to reach the keyboard of the harpsichord. His father, Leopold, plays the violin and his sister, Maria Anna, sings in this water color by the French draftsman Louis de Carmontelle.

OVERLEAF: *At the age of ten, Mozart played for the guests at an English-style tea party in Paris.*

21

whether he loved music or not. It was his life from the start, but it was imposed on him to an extent that aroused his naturally rebellious nature. Few of Ludwig's biographers have been kind to Johann, who was a severe taskmaster, at times returning drunk from the local tavern to awaken his sleeping son and force him to practice until dawn at the clavier or violin. Relaxation was not part of Ludwig's daily schedule.

At times Johann falsified Ludwig's birth date, claiming 1772 instead of 1770. This may have been an honest error. Or he may have done so in order to make Ludwig appear younger and therefore more remarkable—more like Mozart. He was not a completely selfless father; yet however stern his methods, they did mold one of the greatest composers the world has known.

Ludwig began to learn to play the pianoforte at the age of four; his father was his first teacher. As Johann's sober moments became more infrequent, however, various of his father's colleagues played an increasingly important role in the young boy's training as a pianist. The boy also took organ lessons at six in the morning at a Franciscan monastery in Bonn. He learned how to perform so well on that difficult instrument that his teacher soon began to employ him as a substitute organist, probably when Beethoven was no more than nine or ten.

In 1778 Johann arranged for his son to give a concert in Bonn. Ludwig was represented as being two years younger than he actually was, but since no other details are known, it seems probable that he did not make a particularly strong showing as a Mozartlike prodigy.

About that time, the family fortunes were at a low ebb. His father no longer was a capable teacher and knew it. Magdalena even had to sell some of her clothing in order to pay her husband's debts. Anxious to hire qualified teachers for Ludwig, Johann asked the Prince Elector for a raise in salary. But it was not granted, probably because the elder Beethoven had become undependable. Desperate, Johann brought his son to the palace to audition for a position as a court musician. Although he was not given a salary, Ludwig was permitted to participate in some musical events: he played, for example, in the theatre orchestra, probably as a violist. His exposure to the musicians of the court provided him with a disorganized education, but a musical education it was.

In 1781 the famous composer and conductor Christian Gottlob Neefe became Court organist in Bonn. Strolling

AVERTISSEMENT.

Heut dato den 26ten Märtii 1778. wird auf dem musikalischen Akademiesaal in der Sternengaß der Churköllnische Hoftenorist BEETHOVEN die Ehre haben zwey seiner Scholaren zu produciren; nämlich: Madlle. Averdonc Hofaltistin, und sein Söhngen von 6. Jahren. Erstere wird mit verschiedenen schönen Arien, letzterer mit verschiedenen Clavier-Concerten und Trios die Ehre haben aufzuwarten, wo er allen hohen Herrschaften ein völliges Vergnügen zu leisten sich schmeichlet, um je mehr da beyde zum größten Vergnügen des ganzen Hofes sich hören zu lassen die Gnade gehabt haben.

Der Anfang ist Abends um 5. Uhr.

Die nicht abbonnirte Herren und Damen zahlen einen Gulden.

Die Billets sind auf ersagtem musikalischen Akademiesaal, auch bey Hrn. Claren auf der Bach im Mühlenstein zu haben.

Beethoven's first public performance took place on March 26, 1778, at five in the afternoon. Although in fact he was in his eighth year, the announcement claimed that the young clavier player was only six.

through the palace one day, he came upon the young Beethoven at the organ, attempting to play one of Neefe's own difficult compositions. Ludwig was having trouble with it, but only because his hands were not yet large enough to span the necessary keys. Neefe commented that the boy was not yet ready to play that piece. "But I shall when I'm grown," said Beethoven confidently and thus made an important friend.

In 1782 Neefe had to leave Bonn briefly. By then, he already had been convinced that Beethoven was a competent, even brilliant musician; and he had the boy substitute for him as organist in his absence. On his return he increased Ludwig's responsibilities and taught him as much music as the eager youth could absorb. Beethoven played the organ, piano, viola, violin; he arranged trios, improvised at the clavier, and on occasion even rehearsed the orchestra when Neefe was out of town.

In an official report for the Prince, Neefe wrote: "A son

Augustusburg, the Prince Elector's summer palace, pictured above, was situated halfway between Bonn and Cologne, the towns he ruled.

Christian Gottlob Neefe, the court organist at Bonn, became one of Beethoven's earliest admirers.

of Beethoven . . . receives no wage, but took over the organ during the organist's absence; is very capable, still young, of good, decent behavior and is poor.''

In 1783 Neefe further publicized his pupil's talent in the *Magazin der Musik*, an authoritative musical journal: "This youthful genius is deserving of help to enable him to travel. He would surely become a second Wolfgang Amadeus Mozart were he to continue as he has begun.''

A year later, Prince Elector Maximilian Franz, successor to Max Friedrich, gave Ludwig an allowance and officially made him a court musician.

Little is known about Beethoven's life between 1784 and 1787; in all probability, it was routine. Whatever the details, however, he emerged from those three years the independent, stubborn, passionate personality he would remain. One acquaintance described the adolescent Ludwig as "shy and monosyllabic, more observing and thoughtful than he appeared.''

He observed the Court, and he despised it. He did not necessarily hate the courtiers, but he had no patience with courtly manners and no belief in the right of princes to rule other men. Beethoven once reportedly launched into a harangue against royalty before the Prince Elector Maximilian Franz. When Court guards approached to silence him, the Prince Elector said, so the story goes, "Let the young man rave. When he matures he'll be greater than any of you."

Later, to another royal patron, Beethoven would say: "What you are, you are through accident and birth. What I am, I am through my own efforts. There are princes and there will be thousands of princes more, but there is only one Beethoven!"

That, apparently, is what he came to believe in those three years, and he was right.

MAXIMILIANVS ARCH.AVST.
M. Mag. Ord. Teut. Coadj. Archiep.
et Elect. Colon. et Ep. Monast. & &.

Prince Elector Maximilian Franz was the first to pay the young Beethoven a salary for playing.

27

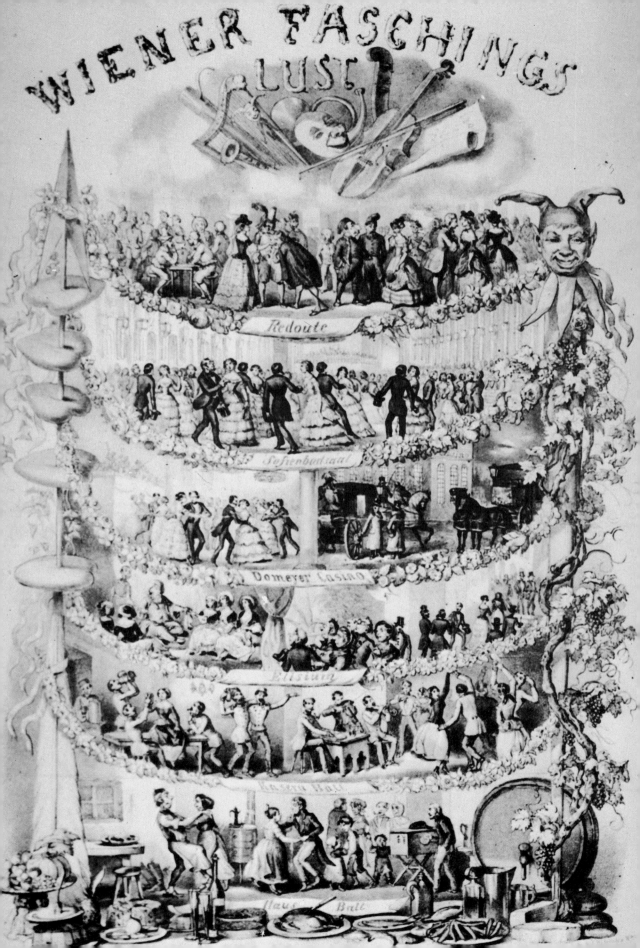

II A SECOND MOZART?

From his three quiet years as court musician to the Elector of Cologne, Beethoven emerged a virtuoso pianist and organist and a composer of promise. But as a man he had acquired no more polish, no better manners than he had had before. Uncultivated, at times withdrawn and at times outgoing and even boisterous, he was a die-hard, testy republican who liked to flaunt his disregard for rank: nobody was his better. But despite his social ineptitude, his brashness, gruffness, and occasional crudeness, he was in his way an attractive youth. He was sixteen through most of 1787, independent and cocksure, almost always in love, and able to attract and hold the attention and affection of a circle of sophisticated, noble friends.

Outside Bonn, however, the name Beethoven was scarcely a household word. Those few old-timers who might have heard it probably thought of Ludwig's grandfather, the *Kapellmeister*. Haydn, Neefe, the sons of Bach, and above all, Mozart—these, in the music-loving German and Austrian principalities of the late eighteenth century, were as universally familiar as the names of professional athletes and astronauts are today.

Ironically, in 1787 Wolfgang Amadeus Mozart was living in Vienna largely on the reputation he had earned as a child. Although he had only four more years to live, he was still young—thirty-one; moreover, he was as prolific as ever and was in the process of composing his greatest works, including the opera *Don Giovanni*. He had, as a correspondent for the *Magazin der Musik* reported, "a decided leaning to what is difficult and unusual. But on the other hand," the writer admitted graciously, "how great and noble

The Viennese knew how to enjoy themselves in Beethoven's time no less than today. The year's frivolity reached its peak during Fasching, *or pre-Lenten carnival season, as this contemporary engraving illustrates. Then balls were held in private houses and public places throughout the city.*

All Vienna mingled in the Prater, a two-thousand-acre park by the Danube.

This colored etching of the airy square known as the High Market was made two years after Beethoven moved to Vienna for good. The monument at the center is a fountain called the Nuptials of the Virgin.

are his ideas, how daring a spirit is displayed in them!"

With these perhaps unintentionally patronizing words, the correspondent (who was not Viennese) seemed to be explaining to his readers why the Viennese apparently had abandoned Mozart. It was true that they still spoke lovingly of him as the Master. It was true that his works were the standard by which all others were judged. But the Viennese did not like to acknowledge that Mozart, the one-time child prodigy, was now an adult, writing "difficult and unusual" music. As a result, they—and their Emperor, Joseph II— neglected him shamefully.

In Bonn in 1787, however, Mozart still represented the ideal of musical genius; and since the advancement of the sixteen-year-old Beethoven had become a sort of personal quest for both his teacher, Neefe, and his patron, the Prince Elector, they decided that it was time for their protégé to call on the Master.

Vienna was much larger, busier, and more international than Bonn. In the 1780's the population exceeded 175,000 —Germans, Latins, Slavs—in their diversity forming, more

When the Austrian emperor Joseph II died in 1790, Beethoven wrote a funeral cantata in his memory. However, it was not performed until 1884.

or less harmoniously, that unique and almost legendary citizenry known as the Viennese. In sharp contrast to courtly little Bonn, Vienna was an industrial city, a flourishing commercial center where manufacturers, artisans, and traders from many countries converged to profit from the well-distributed prosperity.

For all its cosmopolitanism, Vienna was an exception among Europe's capitals in that the revolutionary fervor building up elsewhere was almost totally absent. To an extent, this reflected the success of Emperor Joseph II, the Hapsburg prince who was genuinely anxious to be a "modern" ruler. Foreseeing that some sort of revolution was not only inevitable but also desirable, he hoped that it could be a bloodless one guided from the palace itself. He instituted needed social reforms, surrounded himself with advisors dedicated to democratic ideals, and became, in sum, the most effective practitioner of the philosophy of monarchy called enlightened despotism.

It appears probable, however, that Joseph's success was due as much to the character and traditions of his people as to the enlightenment of his despotism. For in Vienna, as in few other cities on the Continent, overabundance had long been a way of life. If the inhabitants lacked certain individual liberties, they hardly had time or cause to worry about it. The standard of living—thanks mainly to the fertile fields around the city and to the commerce within—was very high, and the cost of living, for the same reasons, very low. Visitors often were struck, or even appalled, by the sheer quantity of everything. Life in the city appeared to consist of eating, walking to aid digestion, and attending a concert or the opera to whet the appetite for another meal. Everyone looked plump, cheerful, lazy—and the Viennese would ask, Why not? It cost little to live and live well: even the beggars, it was pointed out to strangers, were well off. The pace was slow, the attitude cheerful. People who are hungry and whose children are in rags need freedom of speech to complain. Most Viennese probably did not know whether the freedom to speak out was theirs or not, and it probably never occurred to them to ask, for there was little to complain about.

If anything, the prevailing political attitude in Vienna at the time of Beethoven's arrival in the spring of 1787 was one of "Don't rock the boat." It may even be—and this is speculation—that his blunt rebelliousness and brash manner impressed no one in gentle Vienna; for the fact is that his brief visit was not recorded in any of the newspapers or

The Upper Belvedere housed the emperor's picture collection when this print was made in 1785. It remains today the finest baroque garden palace in central Vienna.

in any surviving diary. However, he did get to see Mozart at least once, and the occasion was described, some years after the event, by Mozart's friend and biographer, Jahn:

Beethoven, who as a youth of great promise came to Vienna . . . , was taken to Mozart and at that musician's request played something for him which he, taking it for granted that it was a show-piece prepared for the occasion, praised in a rather cool manner. Beethoven observing this, begged Mozart to give him a theme for improvisation. He always played admirably when excited and

now he was inspired, too, by the presence of the master whom he reverenced greatly; he played in such a style that Mozart, whose attention and interest grew more and more, finally went silently to some friends who were sitting in an adjoining room, and said, vivaciously, "Keep your eyes on him; some day he will give the world something to talk about."

Beethoven may have taken a few lessons from Mozart, but nothing more is known for certain about his visit except that about three months after his arrival he received a series of letters from Bonn, informing him that his mother was ill. Hurrying home, he ran out of money in Augsburg, where a Councillor von Schaden lent him the funds to complete his trip. He arrived in Bonn barely in time to watch Magdalena die—and to see his father reduced to selling some of the family belongings and pawning others. For the time being anyway, Beethoven had to postpone whatever hopes he may have had of settling in Vienna.

In the autumn Beethoven wrote to Schaden in Augsburg. His letter—the earliest surviving one from Beethoven's pen—reveals a great deal about the young man's state of mind:

I can easily imagine what you must think of me, and I can not deny that you have good grounds for an unfavorable opinion [probably for the delay in returning the loan]. I shall not, however, attempt to justify myself, until I have explained to you the reasons why I hope my apologies will be accepted. I must tell you that from the time I left Augsburg my cheerfulness as well as my health began to decline; the nearer I came to my native city the more frequent were the letters from my father urging me to travel with all possible speed, as my mother was not in a favorable state of health. I therefore hurried forward as fast as I could, although myself far from well. . . . I found my mother still alive but in the most deplorable state; her disease was consumption, and about seven weeks ago, after much pain and suffering, she died. She was such a kind, loving mother to me, and my best friend. Ah, who was happier than I when I could still utter the sweet name, mother, and it was heard? And to whom can I now speak it? Only to the silent image resembling her evoked by the power of the imagination. I have passed very few pleasant hours since my arrival here, having during the whole time been suffering from asthma, which may, I fear, eventually develop into consumption; to this is added melancholy—almost as great an evil as my malady itself. Imagine yourself in my place, and then I shall hope to receive your forgiveness for my long silence. You showed me extreme kindness and friendship by lending me three Carolins in Augsburg, but I must entreat your indulgence for a time. My journey cost me a great deal, and I have not the smallest hopes of earning anything here. Fate is not propitious to me in Bonn.

Pardon my detaining you so long with my chatter; it was necessary for my justification.

I do entreat you not to deprive me of your valuable friendship; nothing do I wish so much as in some degree to become worthy of your regard.

I am, with the highest respect
Your most obedient servant and friend,
L. v. Beethoven,
Court Organist to the Elector of Cologne.

Strength and power characterized the young Beethoven's profile and the extraordinary virtuosity with which he played the pianoforte.

Beethoven's letter does not read like that of a sixteen-year-old. He was genuinely sad at his mother's death and weighed down by responsibilities. Even the references to his ill health sound like the hypochondria of an old man. The letter also reveals two other traits that were developing strongly in the young musician: the great value he placed on friendship and his eternal fatalism. Here, of course, his reference to "fate" is not particularly startling: anyone might have used the word to imply that a city held very little of potential value to him. Over the years, however,

37

Beethoven developed what practically amounted to a personal philosophy about the conflict between man and fate.

Beethoven once recalled that his last years in Bonn—1787 until 1792—were the happiest of his life. Perhaps nostalgia, or perhaps some unrecorded event—a love affair, for example—made the years seem worthwhile. But from the details that are known emerges a bleak picture of a responsible but not especially stable youth struggling with too many obligations: a drunken father, two untalented younger brothers, a supremely demanding profession, and the direst poverty.

After the death of his wife Johann van Beethoven let himself go. Habitually intoxicated, he no longer functioned as musician or father; and Ludwig petitioned the Prince Elector, asking that half of Johann's salary be paid directly to him for the education of his brothers. The Court responded favorably and even ordered Johann to leave Bonn. Although the order probably was a warning, and not meant to be taken seriously, thereafter Johann played no substantial part in his sons' lives.

On the other hand, it is only fair to admit that Ludwig was not much of a guardian either. Since 1784, Beethoven had been closer to the Breunings, a noble Bonn family, than to his own. He tutored two of Frau von Breuning's children

Silhouettes from the Bonn years show Beethoven at sixteen, above, just at the time of his friendship with the Breuning family, right. Eleonore stands listening as her mother reads; Lorenz, Beethoven's other Breuning pupil, plays the violin for his uncle; Christoph reads; and Stephan, the composer's friend in later years, plays with the family's pet canary.

in piano and spent a good deal of his time in their house.

Life with the Breunings was pleasant and romantic: Beethoven appeared to fancy himself alternately in love with Frau von Breuning and with the Breuning daughter, Eleonore, to whom he may have proposed marriage. The proposal was refused, as Beethoven's proposals usually were, apparently with little effect on the spirit of the composer. (Eleonore later married Beethoven's closest friend, Doctor Franz Gerhard Wegeler.)

Beethoven did not seem to be in a hurry to publish his own compositions. His "Breuning period" was devoted mostly to cultivating his aristocratic friends and his reputation as a virtuoso on the piano. (He met, most importantly, Count Waldstein, who remained one of his major patrons for many years.)

Beethoven's style as a composer, however, was emerging very clearly in his style as a virtuoso. The prevailing fashion in pianoforte playing at this time was based superficially on the approach of Mozart. Actually, Mozart's manner had been delicate and graceful, never showy, but often subtly dramatic. Imperceptive imitators of the Master's style had distorted that approach and created a fashion that was in fact prim and somewhat ladylike (which Mozart's playing never was). Beethoven detested the style. Once, in 1789, he

was taken to the monastery at Aschaffenburg, where one of Germany's most famous pianists, Abbé Sterkel, lived. Beethoven listened to the monk play for a while, then, as was customary when a youthful musician was confronted with the example of an elder, he took his turn. He precisely duplicated the Abbé's style. Those listeners who had heard Beethoven play before were astonished that he could do it— his own style was anything but delicate.

Ludwig was from all accounts a magnificent pianist. His first public performances shocked many of his audience because his playing was so strong and dramatic: delicacy was for him an exception, not the rule, and his style seemed to contradict all that was held correct in playing at the time. But Bonn provided sophisticated audiences that knew their music extremely well.

Before long, the dynamic Beethoven style had made converts of the flexible listeners and set the traditionalists to reconsidering stylistic canons that they had considered inflexible. Most impressive of all was his brilliant improvising —and like most musicians who are basically composers, he liked best to improvise. One listener described his own reaction to one of young Beethoven's performances:

When [Beethoven] had completely given himself up to the power of his imagination, he would gradually draw away from the magic of merely brilliant passages, and, with the fire of youth, would boldly launch out into distant keys. I was greatly touched by his tremendous excitement. Then, by means of daring modulations, the whole piece would take on a new direction and come to the most heavenly theme. Then another change would come—a mood of sweet sadness, then one of touching delicacy, which in time became joyous. Yet the most complete order prevailed throughout this performance. It was like bright noonday.

The listener might have been describing the compositions of the mature Beethoven, although it would in fact be many years before they were composed.

In 1792 Beethoven left Bonn for Vienna once again, this time to study with the renowned Joseph Haydn. His move to the Austrian capital was financed by Prince Elector Max Franz, who also granted him an allowance during his indefinite leave of absence from the Electoral Court.

Beethoven once sent Eleonore von Breuning this greeting card with the sentiment, in French, "Be as happy as you are beloved." The two remained affectionate friends after her marriage and until the composer's death.

Now Beethoven was ready to begin his career as a "second Mozart"—as his teacher, Neefe, had suggested he would be. And now two events had made Vienna ripe for the moody and confident young genius. Less than a year earlier, Mozart had died at the age of thirty-five. Not only had it been a tragic, senseless death, hastened by overwork and poverty, but Vienna's final tribute to the Master had been a disgrace as well: only five people had attended his funeral. Now the intensely musical city needed another brilliant composer to call its own.

The second event made Beethoven the ideal artist for his time. Mozart had been the darling of the rococo age, when Europe's courts had prized prettiness, gentility, delicacy. He had been perfect for such an era. But as Beethoven—earthy, arrogant, and tough—packed his bags for his journey from the Rhine to the Danube, the army of the French Revolution was crossing the same Rhine and entering Germany farther to the south.

Mozart's disgraceful third-class funeral took place in the rain, and he shared an unmarked grave with a dozen other near-paupers.

With the soldiers marched a new age; soon they would have a new and dynamic leader. And Beethoven's personality would prove perfect for the new age of Napoleon.

Beethoven marched through Vienna's politest drawing rooms as though he were tramping across an open field. Yet when he played, his aristocratic hosts were entranced and forgave everything.

JEU DE QUILLES REPUBLICAIN.

III VIRTUOSO IN VIENNA

Shortly after he arrived in Vienna, Beethoven inscribed these lines in a friend's autograph album:

> I am not wicked—fiery blood
> Is all my malice, and my crime is youth.
> Wicked I am not, truly I am not wicked;
> Though wild up-surgings often may plead against my
>   heart,
> My heart is good.—
> To help wherever one can,
> Love liberty above all things,
> Never deny the truth
> Even at the foot of the throne!

The sentiments expressed in these ungraceful verses were not extraordinary ones in Europe in 1792, for the aims of the French Revolution had captured the sympathy of people everywhere on the Continent. But in Vienna the love of liberty and devotion to the truth even in defiance of the monarchy were still less than universal. In fact, the Viennese were so appalled by the Revolution that they were quite prepared to let their city become the capital of the European anti-Revolution.

The vast majority of the Viennese believed in their rulers —or at least, in their rulers' right to rule. Their attitude toward their monarchs has been compared to that of a normally secure child toward his parents: he may habitually make fun of them, periodically resent them, at times even dislike them; but he also depends on them, and for the most part he trusts them and acknowledges their authority. Moreover, the people of this peaceful city on the Danube liked their monarchs to look and behave like monarchs in the grand manner. Autocratic and stern in a motherly way,

Europe's rulers, like ninepins, wait for the hero of the French Revolution. Liberty holds a wreath, and an angel trumpets the rights of man, while the many-headed specter of counterrevolution lurks in the rocks.

45

The court painter Martin van Mytens chose the balcony of the summer palace at Schönbrunn as the setting for this portrait of Maria Theresa, her
husband, Emperor Francis I, and their thirteen surviving children. The
1,441-room palace, begun in 1694, was the Empress' favorite residence.

Mars looks on while Frederick the Great of Prussia makes a move in the lifelong diplomatic chess game he played with Maria Theresa.

Empress Maria Theresa, who had died in 1780, had been far more popular among the Viennese than her son and successor, Joseph II, the enlightened prince who had done so much to introduce liberal reforms into Austrian political affairs. Indeed, Joseph's modesty and temperance had been so little appreciated that the aristocracy, the clergy, and even the common people often had accused him of being a "crowned revolutionary."

When the Revolution erupted in Paris in 1789, the Viennese genuinely seemed frightened that their own Emperor had had a hand in it, and Joseph actually had to repeal many of his reforms in order to appease his subjects. This very nearly broke his heart: writing to his brother and successor, Leopold II, Joseph confessed that he was "the most distressed of mortals. . . . You know my fanaticism— the word is not too strong—for the public weal, to which I have sacrificed everything. . . . Pity me, dear brother, and may God preserve you from such a fate."

Joseph died in 1790, and Leopold, to preserve himself from the disapproval of the Viennese, pointedly withdrew the remaining democratic elements that his brother had introduced into Austrian law. Condemning the Revolution, he assumed the bearing and the close control of the affairs of state expected of a monarch; and the Viennese were grateful. Two years later, Leopold died, but his anti-Revolutionary policies were adopted and intensified by his successor, Francis II.

Shortly after Francis' accession Vienna began to prepare for the festivities that customarily attend the corona-

Holy Roman Emperor Francis II is shown in 1792 proceeding in the state coach to his coronation in St. Stephan's Cathedral. During his long reign he continued the autocratic policies of his predecessor, Leopold II, reversing the liberal reforms of Joseph II.

48

tion of a new emperor. Francis, however, abruptly asked that the preparations be abandoned. This was, he said, no time for rejoicing. Hysteria, mass executions, near-anarchy were rampant in Paris, and the Revolutionary plague threatened to spread throughout Europe. Saddest of all, the Emperor reminded his subjects, the beloved Austrian princess Marie Antoinette—the daughter of Maria Theresa, wife of Louis XVI, and thus Queen of France—had been condemned by the Revolution and probably would die. Francis felt that mourning was more fitting than celebration. The Viennese caught on readily and enjoyed a period of national mourning for the Revolution that wrapped the city in an atmosphere of unaccustomed gloom.

If Beethoven was conscious of the depression when he arrived in Vienna in 1792, he left no record of it. If he sus-

During her trial a juror named Prieur sketched the portrait of Marie Antoinette reproduced below, left. On October 16, 1793, she was guillotined and her head was paraded before the crowd.

pected that the frightened aristocrats of the city, his prospective benefactors, might resent it if he treated them as equals, he did not alter his behavior in order to win their approval. Neither humble nor subservient, he really did not have to argue out loud in favor of the aims of the Revolution because he was its living, walking, arrogantly bellowing personification: a rebel.

Unlike many Europeans who vocally championed the Revolution, Beethoven had a great deal to lose by expressing his sentiments; the advancement of his career depended to a great extent on the approval of the very people whose positions he desired to see overturned. Beethoven's move to Vienna in order to study with Haydn had been financed by the Prince Elector of Cologne, who also granted him an allowance. Nevertheless, when the French Revolutionary

Beethoven's Opus No. 1, three trios for pianoforte, violin, and cello, was dedicated to his patron Prince Lichnowsky. When Haydn found fault with the composer's favorite trio, Beethoven believed that the older man was jealous.

army approached Bonn not long after Beethoven's departure, and ultimately forced the Elector to flee, Beethoven did not renounce his republican views, despite the fact that the deposition of the Prince meant the end of his allowance.

(Prince Elector-Archbishop Maximilian Franz, incidentally, was welcomed back by his subjects when the French withdrew to deal with troubles at home. In 1794, however, they returned to Bonn and deposed the Prince Elector for the last time. By this time, Beethoven seems to have almost completely forgotten the town of his birth.)

Not surprisingly, Beethoven's lessons with Haydn did not go well. Haydn was a gentle, polite Court composer of the old school—the antithesis of Beethoven. According to one account, the aging master wanted his student to write "Pupil of Haydn" on his manuscripts, which Beethoven refused to do. When Beethoven performed his first three trios (later published as Opus 1), Haydn liked least the one that Beethoven liked best, making the young composer suspect his teacher of jealousy. But even when their teacher-student relationship ended, the past and future masters maintained cordial relations.

Young Beethoven successfully made his way through the drawing rooms of Viennese society, although his methods of courting the aristocrats were extraordinary, to say the least. He arrived late for dinner and demanded a seat at the head table; he was oversensitive, and the slightest comment, perhaps intended as a joke, might trigger his explosive temper. His virtuosity on the piano was such that his audiences often were moved to tears; yet when he finished a performance, he was likely—for no apparent reason—to denounce all his listeners as unspeakable fools. "This is not what we artists wish—we want applause," he reportedly said. His conceit was boundless. Prince Lobkowitz, one of his most faithful patrons, once admonished him for his rudeness to a person who had suggested that Beethoven could not yet call himself Haydn's equal as a composer. Beethoven replied, "With men who do not believe in me because I am not famous, I cannot associate."

Although he gave talent its due, the young virtuoso had little patience with mediocrity. When an average musician was performing, Beethoven often talked aloud or walked about the room or flipped the pages of his own score loudly enough for all to hear. Yet as a performer, he would not tolerate inattention. According to one recollection, he once was playing a piano duet with his friend and pupil Ferdinand Ries; across the room a young nobleman persisted in speaking to a lady. Presently, Beethoven stopped playing, abruptly lifted Ries' hands from the keyboard, and shouted, "I will not play for such swine!" There were apologies and pleas for him to continue, but he absolutely refused. Another time the noted musician Friedrich Himmel sat down at the piano to improvise. After Himmel had played for some time, Beethoven interrupted to ask him when he was going to begin.

(An off-again, on-again friend to Beethoven, Himmel eventually got his revenge. Writing to Beethoven some years later from Berlin, Himmel described a wonderful lamp he had seen that had been invented especially for use by the blind. The gullible Beethoven was impressed and enthusiastically described the wonderful invention to a number of friends.)

Notwithstanding his deplorable manners, Beethoven immediately won a wide circle of aristocratic friends and patrons in Vienna. Baron von Zmeskall virtually became

The composer at the age of thirty-three, in a miniature painted on ivory

Beethoven's valet as well as one of his most lasting friends. "Mr. Muckcart-driver," the musician called the aristocrat, or "Baron Ba . . . ron ron/nor/orn/rno/onr—," a nonsense name that Beethoven apparently thought hysterically funny. One of the Baron's principal roles in the musician's life was to cut the pens that Beethoven used for writing music. Count Browne, an Irishman, gave Beethoven a horse, which he enjoyed for a ride or two and then forgot; the poor animal would have starved to death but for a groom who noticed its sad condition and assumed the responsibility for feeding it.

The aristocrats of Vienna put up with Beethoven's antics and enjoyed or overlooked his eccentricities chiefly because they recognized his genius. These princes, counts, and dukes were themselves musicians—not casual, Sunday-afternoon players but serious, knowledgeable, hard-working musicians who regularly practiced and composed. Indeed, in this most remarkable city, a passion for music united the nobles at least as much as did politics and perhaps more. Some of them held frequent concerts in their houses, and many others were accomplished players in chamber music groups.

For these sophisticated patrons Beethoven composed some of his greatest and most challenging works. His symphonies, his opera *Fidelio*, and the concertos came to be known for their enormous energy and theatricality. His chamber music, on the other hand, which was composed mostly for the nobles who supported him, eventually would be regarded by most professional musicians and critics as his most splendid music. The string quartets in particular often have been cited for their remarkable beauty. Frequently difficult to perform, they achieve all the drama, all the range, and all the subtlety of the great orchestral works; in other words, they accomplish a great deal with relatively little. However harsh the composer's attitude toward the aristocrats—and he could be unmerciful—his chamber works contradict his bitter words: they are actually supreme compliments to the musical understanding and technical expertise of the Viennese nobility.

Beethoven's talent, then, was the primary source of his success in Vienna. However, when considering the favorable attitude of the aristocrats toward the young composer, it is important to recognize his unique personal magnetism. For all his clumsiness and uncouthness, Beethoven was an enormously compelling man. People gathered around him, competed for his attention, seemed almost to wish to be insulted by him. He used people and they knew it: "Never show to men the contempt they deserve," he once wrote, "one never knows to what use one may want to put them."

He regarded friends as "mere instruments on which, when it pleases me, I play; but they can never become noble witnesses of my inner and outer activity, nor be in true sympathy with me; I value them according as they are useful to me." It was remarkable how much abuse his acquaintances would take just to remain in favor with him. "Do not come to me any more," he wrote to a companion one day; "You are a false fellow, and the Devil take all such." To the same friend he wrote the next day, "You are an honorable fellow, and I see you were right. So come this afternoon to me. You will also find Schuppanzigh [a renowned violinist], and both of us will bump, thump, and pump you to your heart's delight." For Beethoven this about face was not unusual: he consistently condemned and banished his closest friends, yet expected them to be available and utterly devoted to him a moment later.

His magnetism, which was apparently fully operative even before he became a successful composer, seems to have worked on women, too—though only up to a point. His closest friend, Wegeler, wrote that "Beethoven was always in

Marie-Thérèse von Brunsvik was Beethoven's pupil and one of his many loves. Her father, Count Anton, was her teacher's patron.

love and made many conquests which would have been difficult if not impossible for many an Adonis." Yet the women he loved seemed to recognize the fiery, introspective nature that made him an unsuitable prospect for a husband. He proposed marriage often and each time was refused. Giulietta Guicciardi probably refused his proposal; so, too, did Marie-Thérèse von Brunsvik. Giulietta was the niece, and Marie-Thérèse the daughter of a patron, Count Anton von Brunsvik. The rejections did not seem to disturb him significantly, although the prospect of life without a permanent partner sometimes did. "Now you can help me to look for a wife. . . ." he wrote to a patron. "But she must be good looking; I cannot love anything that is not beautiful."

Beethoven's profoundest emotions probably could find expression only in musical terms. His logic was the logic of music, his vocabulary the vocabulary of musical notation. He might speak glowingly of nature, assert his eagerness to love and be loved, proclaim his devotion to the ideals of the Revolution, but his real and most revealing emotions were expressed most articulately in his music, not in words.

In the last years of the eighteenth century Beethoven's emotions tended to be high-spirited ones. He had lost the

For a time Beethoven was romantically linked to another pupil, Giulietta Guicciardi, a first cousin of Marie-Thérèse's. To her he dedicated the sonata whose title page appears below, better known now as the Moonlight Sonata.

Beethoven spent several years as an honored and pampered guest in the house of Prince Karl Lichnowsky, the faithful patron whose portrait appears at left.

allowance from the Elector in Bonn, but his new patrons in Vienna were filling his pockets and stomach. The singer Magdalena Willmann had refused his written proposal of marriage—she reportedly did not even reply. But Beethoven's social life was full and entertaining. If he wore them carelessly, his clothes were nonetheless stylish; he learned to dance (badly); he was invited to many of the most fashionable afternoon garden parties and evening music parties. Indeed, for several years he lived as a guest in the house of Prince Karl Lichnowsky, an extremely talented amateur musician and one of Beethoven's more faithful patrons.

In Lichnowsky's house a number of Beethoven's works were tested by the quartet that the prince hired for his Friday evening concerts. According to Wegeler, Beethoven "always listened with pleasure" to the criticisms of the players and the noble members of the prince's circle who made up the audience. Lichnowsky ordered his servants to answer a summons from the composer before answering one from him or his princess. In addition, he presented Beethoven with four valuable and excellent Italian stringed instruments and a generous annuity. But for the composer no situation lacked its dark side, and he chafed at the necessity of returning to Lichnowsky's house at three-thirty every afternoon to change and shave before dinner at four.

Beethoven still was known best as a virtuoso, but he was beginning to make his mark as a composer. His first six string quartets were published as a set in 1801 and dedicated to Prince Lobkowitz. They are not unlike those of Haydn and Mozart in style, but a hint of the later Beethoven is apparent throughout: they are moody, powerful, full of surprises, and they seem almost calculated to test to the limit the capabilities of the instruments for which they were composed (two violins, a cello, a viola).

Just as his virtuoso playing of the pianoforte was noted for its strength rather than its delicacy, so, too, were his compositions notable immediately for their driving rhythms and vigor. In the nineteenth century the power evoked by his work would become the dominant element, and the effect of it on the history of music would be profound.

"*Power*," Beethoven once said, "is the morality of men who stand out from the rest, and it is also mine." Power usually is not regarded as a system of morality. It may be a means to achieve a moral end—or an amoral end—but it is not a virtue or a vice in its own right. To a man like Beethoven, however, power meant strength—specifically, the strength to overcome the obstacles laid down by life's principal antagonist: Fate. Power was what made Napoleon the heroic figure he was to Beethoven in the beginning, and the little colonel's later abuse of power as Emperor made him contemptible to the composer.

In 1800 Beethoven was thirty years old. If his life had ended then, he would not have been remembered with any of the reverence accorded Mozart, who died at thirty-five, or Schubert, who died at thirty-one. (Indeed, of all the great composers, Beethoven probably was the least prolific; compared with the output of Bach, Handel, Mozart, Haydn, or Schubert, the list of his works is miniscule.) After 1800, however, he composed more frequently, and the unique character of his work increased. The reason is well known: Beethoven's growing deafness gave him a tragic opportunity to exercise his "morality of power" philosophy.

It probably was in 1798 that Beethoven first noticed that his hearing was deteriorating. For three years he appears to have thought the trouble temporary. In 1801, however, he began to mention it from time to time in his letters. To his good friend Karl Friedrich Amenda he confessed:

Your Beethoven is most unhappy and at strife with nature and Creator. I have often cursed the latter for exposing his creatures to the merest accident, so that often the most beautiful buds are broken or destroyed thereby. Only think that my noblest faculty, my hearing, has greatly deteriorated. . . . Oh, how happy could I be if my hearing were completely restored; then would I hurry to you, but as it is I must refrain from everything and the most beautiful years of my life must pass without accomplishing the promise of my talent and powers. A sad resignation to which I must resort although, indeed, I am resolved to rise superior to every obstacle. But how will that be possible? . . . I beg of you to keep the matter of my deafness a profound secret to *be confided to nobody no matter who it is. . . .*

Later that same month Beethoven wrote to Wegeler, giving more details of his affliction. Yet despite his anguish, his letters show that he had no intention of giving in easily:

. . . my hearing has grown steadily worse for three years. . . . [Dr.] Frank wanted to tone up my body by tonic medicines and restore my hearing with almond oil, but . . . nothing came of the effort; my hearing grew worse and worse. . . . This lasted until the autumn of last year, and I was often in despair. Then came a medical ass who advised me to take cold baths, a more sensible one to take the usual lukewarm Danube bath. That worked wonders; my bowels improved, my hearing remained, or became worse. I was really miserable during this winter; I had frightful attacks of colic and I fell back into my previous condition, and so things remained until about four weeks ago, when I went to Vering, thinking that my condition demanded a surgeon, and having great confidence in him. He succeeded almost wholly in stopping the awful diarrhea. He prescribed the lukewarm Danube bath, into which I had each time to pour a little bottle of strengthening stuff, gave me no medicine of any kind until about four weeks ago, when he prescribed pills for my stomach and a kind of tea for my ear. Since then I can say I am stronger and better; only my ears whistle and buzz continually, day and night. I can say I am living a wretched life; for two years I have avoided almost all social gatherings because it is impossible for me say to people: "I am deaf." If I belonged to any other profession it would be easier, but in my profession it is an awful state. . . . Heaven knows what will happen to me. . . . I have often—cursed my existence. . . . If possible I will bid defiance to my fate, although there will be moments in my life when I shall be the unhappiest of God's creatures. . . .

HISTORISCHES MUSEUM DER STADT WIEN

Prince Franz Joseph von Lobkowitz, Beethoven's patron and almost exact contemporary, lived lavishly in the palace at right, in the center of Vienna. The prince's orchestra frequently performed works by the composer.

Throughout that year and the next, Beethoven went from doctor to doctor, trying anything, collecting stories of miraculous cures: "Miracles are told of *galvanism*," he wrote; ". . . A doctor told me that he had seen a deaf and dumb child recover his hearing again—and a man who had been deaf seven years got well." To Wegeler once more he complains:

Oh, if I were rid of this affliction I could embrace the world! I feel that my youth is just beginning and have I not always been ill? My physical strength has for a short time past been steadily growing more than ever and also my mental powers. Day by day I am approaching the goal which I apprehend but cannot describe. It is only in this that your Beethoven can live. . . . No! I cannot endure it. I will take fate by the throat; it shall not wholly overcome me. Oh, it is so beautiful to live—to live a thousand times!

Realizing that as an artist he was just beginning to approach the prime of his life, he felt that only as an artist

After these and other experiments with frogs' legs, the Italian anatomist Luigi Galvani claimed that there was inherent electricity in animals. For some reason, Beethoven thought that galvanism might help his hearing.

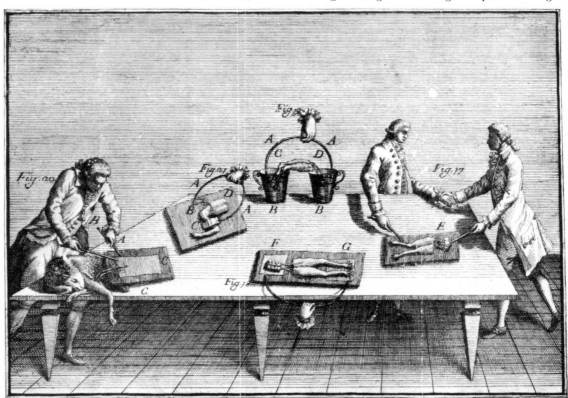

could he survive. He was determined to assert himself, to defend his creative power against ill fortune.

In the summer of 1802, on the advice of still another physician, Dr. Schmidt, Beethoven moved to the little village of Heiligenstadt, not far from Vienna, in order to spare his hearing and take the local mineral baths. All summer he lived alone, took long walks in the Vienna woods, and worked. In the fall it was apparent to him that his hearing was beyond repair, and he contemplated suicide. He even made a will. Discovered long after his death, it is known as the Heiligenstadt Testament; and it was addressed to his brothers, "Carl and _____ Beethoven." (The master had been at odds with brother Johann and still refused to write his name, will or no will.) The Testament clearly represents the lowest point in Beethoven's life:

O ye men who think or say that I am malevolent, stubborn or misanthropic, how greatly do ye wrong me, you do not know the secret causes of my seeming . . . but reflect that for six years I have been in a hopeless case, aggravated by senseless physicians . . . finally compelled to face the prospect of a *lasting malady*. . . .

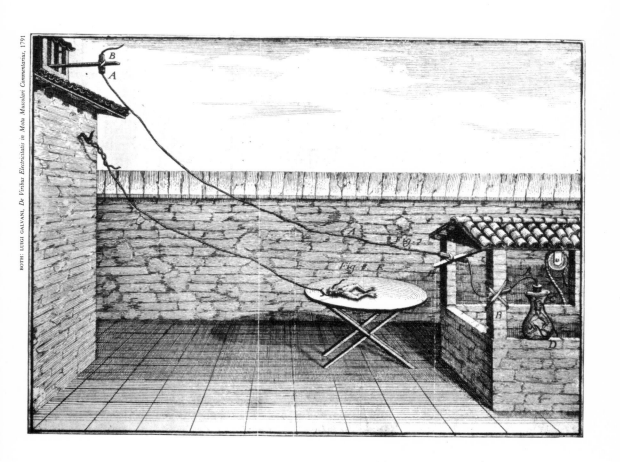

Of the three Beethoven brothers, Johann was the most successful. Six years Ludwig's junior, he made a good living as an apothecary.

O how harshly was I repulsed by the doubly sad experience of my bad hearing, and yet it was impossible for me to say to men speak louder, shout, for I am deaf. Ah how could I possibly admit an infirmity in the one sense which should have been more perfect in me than in others, a sense which I once possessed in highest perfection. . . . what a humiliation when one stood beside me and heard a flute in the distance and *I heard nothing*, or someone heard the *shepherd singing* and again I heard nothing, such incidents brought me to the verge of despair, but little more and I would have put an end to my life—only art it was that withheld me, ah it seemed impossible to leave this world until I had produced all that I felt called upon to produce. . . . will [Death] not free me from a state of endless suffering? Come when thou will I shall meet thee bravely.

Four days later, on October 10, Beethoven added a postscript to the Testament. It seems to indicate that even his will to survive had disappeared.

. . . thus do I take my farewell of thee—and indeed sadly—yes that beloved hope—which I brought with me when I came here to be cured at least in a degree—I must wholly abandon, as the leaves of autumn fall and are withered so hope has been blighted, almost as I came—I go away—even the high courage—which often inspired me in the beautiful days of summer—has disappeared—O Providence—grant me at last but one day of pure joy —it is so long since real joy echoed in my heart—O when, O when, O Divine One—shall I find it again in the temple of nature and men—Never? no—O that would be too hard.

We cannot know what went through Beethoven's head in that tragic autumn of 1802. Needless to say, he did not commit suicide. He completed the Heiligenstadt Testament and returned to Vienna, gripping Fate by the throat, as he said he would. About his change from despair to defiance Beethoven's writings offer no clue.

But his music is an open book.

OVERLEAF: *In Beethoven's time Heiligenstadt was a pastoral village, although it was no more than three miles from the center of Vienna. Today it is actually a suburb of the Austrian capital.*

"A MUSICAL REVOLUTIONARY"

After the summer of his great depression Beethoven began to play less and compose more. And he made really extraordinary progress as a composer. By 1804, only two years after Heiligenstadt, the Viennese already were comparing him to Mozart and Haydn.

Like his two distinguished predecessors, Beethoven belonged to the period of music history called Classic, which lasted from about 1750 to about 1820. During that time, factors both musical and nonmusical speeded the evolution of musical style.

Before the middle of the eighteenth century most music was church music written for the human voice. Instrumental music was composed largely for the pleasure of the musicians themselves or for the entertainment of the nobility at small concerts in small rooms. Public concerts in large auditoriums were almost unheard-of. Only in church were substantial size and volume required—and even then a cantata or a mass was sung by more than six or eight voices only on special occasions.

The growing middle class and the advancing technology of the eighteenth century created, respectively, greater demands for music and the means to satisfy those demands. As their wealth and influence, level of learning and taste grew, the burghers of the European middle class sought to share the culture of the aristocracy. Music was an important part of that culture—in Germany and Austria perhaps even more than elsewhere.

During the Classic period the large public concert became increasingly popular. Filling a public hall with music, however, required larger groups of musicians than had performed chamber music; as a result, larger orchestras came

Beethoven's papier-mâché ear trumpet, one of many with which the deaf composer hoped to hear the music and conversation around him, rests on the manuscripts of two of his greatest symphonies: the third and the ninth.

Above is a facsimile of an Austrian eighteenth-century violin-horn. Holding it vertically, the player could bow and blow simultaneously.

The pianoforte below was built in the Vienna shop of Mattaus Andreas Stein, the brother of Beethoven's friend Nanette Streicher. Their father, Johann Andreas, was not only a noted pianist and organist but also the developer of a pianoforte escapement mechanism called the German movement.

Before the seventeenth century, players of diverse instruments might be called in to provide special effects at concerts, but they did not constitute an orchestra as we know it. Then, with the bowed stringed instruments as the nucleus, sections of wood-winds, brass, and percussion players were added. Composers scored their music to maintain the balance of sound, in effect thinking of the orchestra as a single huge instrument. Below are some of the eighteenth-century German and Austrian instruments that contributed to the growth of the orchestra during Beethoven's time.

Among the predecessors Beethoven particularly admired were the composers Johann Sebastian Bach, left, and George Frederick Handel, above. He was well known in Vienna for his virtuoso playing of Bach's long and difficult work, The Well-Tempered Clavier. *When on his deathbed he was given Handel's complete works, he declared: "I have long wanted them, for Handel is the greatest, the ablest composer that ever lived."*

into being, using the bigger, louder, more versatile instruments that eighteenth century technology developed. In particular, the delicate clavichord and harpsichord were evolving into the more powerful pianoforte, the ancestor of the modern piano. The range of the new instruments challenged the capabilities of the performers; both challenged the inventiveness of the composers. Instrumental music for larger groups of musicians replaced vocal music as the principal interest of many composers, including the three masters of the Classic period.

On the other hand, the Classic composers continued to use the forms familiar to Handel and Bach before them. The difference was the more flexible and more dramatic music that they wrote in those forms. The Classic age was a transitional period between the rigorous observance of form that had characterized Handel and Bach and the relative freedom of form enjoyed by those nineteenth-century composers known as the Romantics. The Classic period in music reflected the contemporary belief that human reason could explain most things but that the imagination of the creative artist was something special and should be respected. Emotion in music began to be important, and it stretched the old forms to their limit. It was his realization of the ultimate in the Classic style that made the Romantics consider Beethoven their most illustrious ancestor.

One of the basic forms of Classic music was the sonata, a structure that had long been known and that proved well suited to large instrumental works. The Classic symphony, typically, is a sonata for orchestra. Many works called string quartets actually are sonatas scored for four stringed instruments.

The Classic sonata was divided into three or four parts, called movements. Characteristically, the first movement was fast (allegro), although it might begin slowly. The themes were presented in the first part of the movement (in what is known as the exposition). Then these themes might be developed in another key by different sections of the orchestra playing them in different rhythms and harmonies. Finally, there was a recapitulation of what had gone before, and sometimes also a coda, or brief summary, to conclude the first movement.

The second movement was usually slow (adagio or andante), although the composer had a good deal of freedom in the way in which he might develop his themes. The third movement was generally a minuet (also allegro), and the last movement was typically the fastest of all (allegro

OVERLEAF: *Haydn last appeared in public in March, 1808, at a performance of his oratorio* The Creation. *This painting, made after a contemporary water color, depicts the scene at Vienna University. Beethoven and the rest of musical Vienna were present at the concert to do honor to Haydn.*

HISTORISCHES MUSEUM DER STADT WIEN

Some months before its first public performance, Beethoven's third symphony was played in this elegant room in the palace of Prince Lobkowitz.

assai or presto). In a sonata composed in only three movements, the minuet sometimes would be omitted.

Beethoven's symphonies seldom depart radically from the sonata form, and when they do, the variations are no greater than those found in the last symphonies of Mozart and Haydn. Nor did Beethoven score his symphonies for orchestras appreciably larger than those used by his two predecessors. Yet because Beethoven, in contrast to Mozart and Haydn, thought of each movement and often of the whole work as an organic unit, his music sounds more emotional, and bigger, as though it were being played by a larger orchestra than actually was used.

As the twentieth-century critic Donald Francis Tovey has written: "It was not Beethoven's forms but his dramatic power that gave him the reputation of a musical revolutionary. Neither in fact nor in . . . opinion could his art forms be regarded as subversive of the principles on which Mozart and Haydn worked. . . ."

Beethoven's "dramatic power" started something new in music. It was the element in his music that made the Romantics think themselves his heirs (as they were). It probably is the element that makes his music so recognizable, so potent, and so widely admired. For if Beethoven's music is dramatic, its drama is a human drama, its power the power of man. This is what has made his works almost always popular, regardless of changing fashions.

Beethoven's first symphony was performed on April 2, 1800, in Vienna. Its debt to the works of Mozart and Haydn was apparent to the audience. Some of its elements probably struck the listeners as unique, however, and not entirely admirable. The very first chord, for instance, was dissonant. The scoring for the wind instruments sounded heavy-handed. Not until the second symphony was presented three years later was the first fully appreciated. Then the listeners realized that Beethoven had chosen to be dissonant, that he wanted the effects of heavy woodwinds.

The third symphony was a real breakthrough. Known as *Eroica*, or "heroic," it announced to the world that Ludwig van Beethoven was a great composer. As music historian David Boyden writes, it "predicts a new world."

What must it have been like for the Viennese who attended the Theater an der Wien on April 7, 1805, when the *Eroica* had its first public performance? At Beethoven's insistence, they had paid unusually high prices for tickets, and they came expecting to hear another of Beethoven's splendid works. They heard a splendid work—but one so strange

and so long that they were not sure that it was music at all.

A contemporary review of the *première* noted that the audience seemed to divide into three groups. The first, Beethoven's friends, felt that the symphony was his masterpiece. The second was typified by a man in the gallery who is reported to have shouted, "I'll give another kreutzer if the thing will but stop!" And the third, while acknowledging that the piece contained many beautiful moments, felt that it was far too long. The review concluded: "The public and Herr van Beethoven, who conducted, were not satisfied with each other on this evening; the public thought the symphony too heavy, too long, and himself too discourteous, because he did not nod his head in recognition of the applause which came from a portion of the audience. On the contrary, Beethoven found the applause was not strong enough."

The third symphony opens starkly, dramatically, almost rudely, with two brief, loud, clipped chords—blasts, really. It is as though the orchestra is scolding: "Quiet! Listen!" The audience is called to attention. Next a fast, dark theme —actually a quotation from an early Mozart opera— emerges as though from the shadows: the whole orchestra is busy, each section almost ignoring the others, the winds apparently beginning their part before the strings have completed theirs, contradicting what the strings are saying. But this is carefully planned complexity, not confusion; the main theme returns, time and again, until it dominates the movement—almost brutally—in what one critic calls "a lengthy and unquotable display of fireworks." After a gigantic crescendo—strings pulsating quickly, woodwinds attempting without success to interject reason, horns blaring the main theme—the orchestra gets together at last for three chords—blasts, again—and the movement closes as abruptly as it began.

The second movement (adagio assai) is a funeral march. If Beethoven never had labeled it a funeral march, it could be that it would have become one anyway. (The Germans to this day broadcast this movement whenever there is a state disaster, as after the Battle of Stalingrad in World War II; in the United States the New York Philharmonic played it on television after the assassination of Senator Robert

Beethoven was for a time the official composer for the Theater an der Wien. A number of his works were played here, including the first really public performance of the Eroica *symphony and of his opera,* Fidelio.

79

Kennedy.) The movement sounds grief-stricken; it seems to sob. The orchestra plods, playing almost unwillingly, almost endlessly. Halfway through, the violins sigh as though in resignation, ready to quit; but immediately the basses and horns interrupt sternly, and the pace quickens as they scold. At this point the key of C minor—which Beethoven so often used to suggest tragedy—gives way to C major, a more hopeful sound. Sorrow remains, but now dignity is mingled with the grief. The march continues: near the end a clock ticks. There is a large, long sob, but it seems more to represent a last outpouring of emotion to wipe clean the slate of sorrow. Life, so to speak, goes on.

The third movement is a scherzo (literally, "joke," but it need not be funny), played quickly, with spirit (allegro vivace). It begins gently, with the strings singing the rhythmic tune, not too loudly, as though they were the advance guard of an army on the move. Almost immediately, the rest of the instruments join in, this time quite loudly. Life has resumed. The force of the scherzo seems indestructible: the main theme recurs time and again, introduced by the fanfarelike horns; each time, the theme returns more strongly and more forcefully than before. By now, the tragic mood of the second movement has been left far behind.

The final movement, played at very fast then moderate speed (allegro molto, poco andante), is a set of variations on a theme used by Beethoven in three previous works. Over and over again the theme is heard—now spirited, now tuneful, now gentle, now plodding. In the slower section the theme virtually is dissected by various instruments, until at last—as though everything that could be learned about it has been learned—the melody fades and the orchestra momentarily murmurs indecisively. Suddenly, the instruments shout in unison: quickly again, louder and louder, the music races on, the original theme absorbed. Faster and faster the *Eroica* speeds to its triumphant conclusion. The symphony seems not so much to end as to move on to an existence too grand to be expressed by musical instruments.

No one can state categorically that the *Eroica* was the greatest symphony ever composed up to 1805, but certainly it was the biggest symphony and probably the most complex. Yet as more than one writer has noted, it is a very compact work: every detail counts.

Perhaps most significantly, the *Eroica* marked a turning point in Beethoven's career as a composer. From then on his work increasingly reflected the quality of dramatic expressiveness that remains a hallmark of his music today.

The second movement of Beethoven's third symphony, shown in manuscript, is a solemn funeral march that elaborates on the basic three-part structure of the song form.

81

V FALLEN IDOL

The *Eroica* was a landmark in the history of music and in the personal and professional development of its creator. It was a testament to the triumph of human will power over fate and an announcement of Beethoven's "arrival" as a composer of profound originality and major importance.

But the *Eroica* also was destined to become, as it has remained, the symbol of an age.

To the millions who have listened to and have been moved by the third symphony the *Eroica* is inseparably associated with Napoleon. Few would suggest that it is in any sense a "musical portrait" of the French emperor and conqueror. Instead, the work is regarded as a musical celebration of the quality of heroism that, in Beethoven's opinion, was exemplified by Napoleon's early career.

The story of the relationship between the *Eroica* and Napoleon has been handed down by Ferdinand Ries. An often abused friend and student of Beethoven's, Ferdinand was the son of Franz Ries, one of the Bonn musicians who had helped educate young Ludwig in his craft when Johann van Beethoven's drinking had threatened the boy's musical progress. Franz had sent his son to Vienna to study with Beethoven from 1801 through 1805. Although Ferdinand became a very successful concert pianist, he spent much of his energy promoting Beethoven's works—particularly in London, where he lived for some years after 1813. (In exchange, Ries received fewer thanks than complaints from his mentor.)

Ries saw Beethoven as frequently as anyone did while the composer was working on the *Eroica*. The master began it during the summer of 1802 at Heiligenstadt and completed it in 1803. While writing the symphony, Ries recalled,

When Napoleon was First Consul of France, as he was when this portrait was made in 1799, he seemed to Beethoven and the other liberals of Europe to champion the ideals of the French Revolution. Only when he became emperor five years thereafter was his image as a democratic leader shattered.

. . . Beethoven had Bonaparte in mind, but as he was when he was First Consul. Beethoven esteemed him greatly at the time and likened him to the greatest Roman consuls. I as well as several of his more intimate friends saw a copy of the score lying upon his table, with the word "Buonaparte" at the extreme top of the title page, and at the extreme bottom "Luigi van Beethoven," but not another word.* Whether and with what the space between was to be filled out, I do not know.

Apparently Beethoven had dedicated the symphony to Napoleon and had intended to insert a dedication message on the page.

Before the third symphony was written, Napoleon had become master of much of the Continent. Although in 1803 his armies had not yet overrun all the principalities of Germany and Austria, many of their rulers were frightened enough to have made peace with Bonaparte—almost always on his terms. Napoleon was limited only by England and the threat of an English alliance with those countries not directly under his control. For the most part, however, Napoleon's will was law in Europe.

The expression of Napoleon's will was embodied in the Napoleonic Code, a series of laws that seemed to codify the aims of the French Revolution. Although in practice the Code sometimes was suspended by Napoleon himself, it guaranteed Europeans certain political and religious freedoms that they had not always had before. The Code won Napoleon a large number of supporters in and out of France, and because of it many European rulers were reluctant to oppose him, knowing that many of their own subjects would welcome Bonaparte in their eagerness to share in the greater personal liberties that he promised.

"Liberty and progress," Beethoven once wrote, "are the goals of art just as life in general." In his view Napoleon was the crusader whose sword would introduce liberty and progress to all the princely states of the Continent. Beethoven was too sure of his own genius to regard Napoleon as the sole hero of the age, but it does seem likely that he

---

*By Beethoven's time, Germany and Austria had become the centers of music in the Western world. Centuries earlier, however, when Italy had held that distinction, the Italians had standardized musical terminology; thus, "fast," "moderate," and "slow" generally are noted *allegro*, *andante*, and *adagio*, and most familiar terms—such as *fortissimo*, "very loud," and *piano*, "soft"—are in the Italian language. It was not unusual for a composer to Italianize all or part of his name on a formal manuscript. Beethoven was unpredictable in this respect, sometimes writing his name "Luigi" and sometimes "Ludwig."

thought of him as a hero. Like Beethoven, Napoleon had mastered fate and boldly defied traditions. Quite probably Beethoven thought of Napoleon and himself as two of a kind. It was reasonable that he should dedicate his "heroic" symphony to Bonaparte.

In 1799 Napoleon was named First Consul of France, a title borrowed from ancient Rome, for France had begun to imagine itself a latter-day Roman Empire. "Consul" was better than "emperor," since in ancient Rome a consul had been an elected official. Emperors, in the popular imagination if not in historical fact, were thought of most frequently as absolute rulers endowed with dictatorial powers.

The citizen-soldiers of the army of republican France plant a "liberty tree" in the center of a German town. The Austrian cartoonist who depicted the scene was understandably somewhat less than charitable to the invaders.

Using this and other sketches he had made, the French painter Jacques Louis David spent three years immortalizing Napoleon's self-coronation in a gigantic oil painting.

In fact, however, the First Consul of France was an absolute ruler. He neither rose to power nor governed by democratic process. His conquests were responsible for his popularity in France; the people gladly consented to his rule because he brought them success and prosperity.

The bubble was burst by Napoleon himself. In May, 1804, the First Consul had himself declared Emperor of France. In addition to the title change, the office was to become hereditary. He no longer would even pretend to be a democratic ruler.

Napoleon's decision came as a blow to many of his admirers. Intelligent people had recognized that he had al-

This was Beethoven's working copy of the title page of his third symphony, known as the Eroica. *There is a note to the copyist at the top of the page, then the words "sinfonia grande." The next line, "intitolata Bonaparte" ("entitled Bonaparte"), has been violently crossed out by the composer.*

ways enjoyed power, had always relished grandeur and his enormous influence. But earlier it could be said that he was a man who simply enjoyed his work—his work being to spread the ideals of the French Revolution. However, no one could expect an emperor to preside over the democratization of Europe. Now an absolute monarch again ruled France and again would march across the Continent.

Ferdinand Ries brought the news of Napoleon's new title to Beethoven. According to Ries, the master "flew into a rage and cried: 'Is he then, too, nothing more than an ordinary human being? Now he, too, will trample on all the rights of man and indulge only his ambition. He will exalt himself above all others, become a tyrant!' Beethoven went to the table, took hold of the top of the title page [of the third symphony], tore it off and flung it on the floor."

Beethoven later replaced the title page with a new one stating simply, "Composed to celebrate the memory of a great man." Many observers have suggested that he still had Napoleon in mind but meant that Napoleon, for Beethoven, was dead.

The dedication may be uncertain, but the music remains. That Beethoven could write such a stirring, triumphant symphony at so bleak a period in his life is in itself an act of heroism. And as a hero, he picked up the loose ends of his fate-stricken life and entered upon the most fruitful period of his career.

Beethoven was a most complex man, heroic at times but also quick-tempered, petty, eccentric, demanding, stubborn. Having brought his two brothers to Vienna, he complained loudly that their sole aim in life was to torture and take advantage of him. It is probably nearer the truth to say that he caused them more heartache than they caused him. Carl, a proud and quick-tempered man, served for a time as Beethoven's secretary and therefore was vulnerable to the composer's stormy moods and unending meddling in Carl's personal affairs. Johann came off somewhat better, for besides successfully practicing a completely different trade— that of druggist—he had something of his brother Ludwig's stubborn independence.

It is difficult to say why Beethoven, so grand in his musical ideas, was so small-minded in other matters. Perhaps he was defiant by nature. He defied authority, he defied rules, he defied fate. And as with many defiant people, he could not tolerate resistance. He had succeeded despite an unfortunate family. He had earned the respect and friendship of the aristocracy while treating them as equals. He had

been cursed by nature with the loss of a musician's most important sense—his hearing—only to rise to unprecedented heights as a composer. His brothers suffered from the affliction of being merely average mortals. Beethoven had risen above mediocrity and therefore felt that he knew better than they—even about things that were their affair, not his. Their failure to admit this infuriated him.

His brothers were right not to permit Beethoven to run their lives. He was a genius, but only as a composer and musician. Otherwise he was a man of average intelligence. Nor was he particularly articulate: his writing was heavy-handed and filled with clichés. Once, in a letter to his friend Wegeler, he explained his delay in replying by saying:

89

"Often I write the answer in my head; yet when I want to set it down I usually throw away my pen, because I am not capable of writing exactly what I feel."

It has been said that Beethoven, of all the great composers, most strongly felt and thought, dreamed, and even joked in the language of music. His verbal humor was crude while in music his wit was subtle and sophisticated. Around 1815, for instance, a number of musicians were using the metronome to indicate tempos. A pendulum device that ticks back and forth at a preset speed, the invention was supposed to ensure that a musical composition would be performed at the exact tempo intended by the composer. (How to determine the fastness of fast [allegro], the slowness of slow [adagio] always has been a problem in music. If you have two recordings of the same piece of music, you probably have noticed the differences. The composer's intention

Copying Beethoven's works was a thankless job: although his writing often was illegible, he blamed the other fellow for mistakes. Here, a copyist dared to defend his work, causing the composer to draw a furious cross through the letter and scrawl on it, "stupid, conceited, asinine fellow." Then Beethoven added at the bottom, "Compliments for such a good-for-nothing, who pilfers one's money? —better to pull his asinine ears."

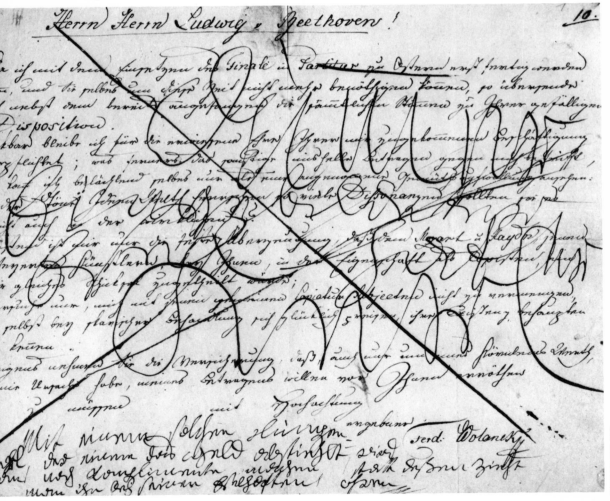

90

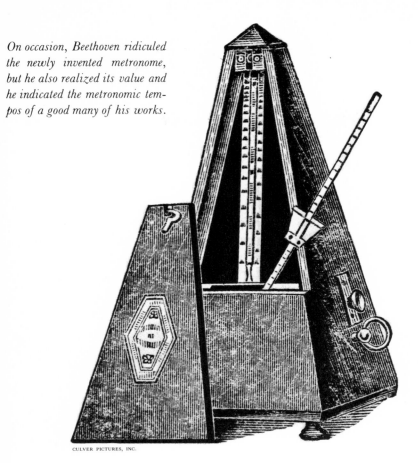

On occasion, Beethoven ridiculed the newly invented metronome, but he also realized its value and he indicated the metronomic tempos of a good many of his works.

CULVER PICTURES, INC.

is always subject to the interpretation of the conductor.)

Beethoven sometimes did mark down the metronome speeds for his pieces. But using it did not prevent him from poking good-humored fun at it. His most memorable comment became part of the scherzo of his eighth symphony. A steady instrumental tick-tick-tick-tick-tick continues through most of the movement, superimposed on the other melody and variations. It is not the knee-slapping kind of humor, but a whimsical musical joke—a parody—on the possible consequences of the metronome tempos.

Beethoven left less than two hundred major works or series of works.* Moreover, writing music never was easy

*Beethoven wrote more than two hundred works, if we count them individually. A composer's works, however, usually are numbered according to their order of publication. If he publishes several related pieces at once, they all are given a single number, or *opus* number. For example, Beethoven's Opus 1, or first published work, is a set of three trios, published in 1795. His famous Opus 18 of 1801 comprises six separate string quartets. But each concerto and symphony represents an individual opus number.

Beethoven, a bachelor, was not a domesticated creature. He spent much of his time at the White Swan Tavern in Vienna's Neumarkt, shown in the water color below, often in the company of his faithful friend Baron Zmeskall. He also would take a pipe in one of the town's many coffeehouses, where he was sketched above in 1823. Or he would walk the streets, note pad in hand, oblivious to everything including the artist drawing him.

for him, and in this he was the complete opposite of Mozart. It is said that Mozart could and often did write out his works at the dinner table, while scarcely missing a word of the conversation. He could work this way because he actually had composed the piece in his head before he sat down to transcribe it. Beethoven wrote in bits and snatches, working on several pieces at once. He kept elaborate notebooks of musical ideas, labored over the scoring and elements of notation, and did a great deal of experimenting at the piano. Then he would repeatedly revise completed manuscripts until the day they went to the printer.

The remarkable paradox is that the more productive and meticulous Beethoven became as a composer, the more disorderly was his day-to-day life. In 1805 Ferdinand Ries records:

In his behavior Beethoven was awkward and helpless; his uncouth movements were often destitute of all grace. He seldom took anything into his hands without dropping and breaking it. Thus he frequently knocked ·his ink-well into the pianoforte which stood near by the side of his writing table. No piece of furniture was safe from him, least of all a costly piece. Everything was overturned, soiled and destroyed. It is hard to comprehend how he accomplished so much as to be able to shave himself, even leaving out of consideration the number of cuts on his cheeks . . .

Beethoven was often extremely violent. One day we were eating our noonday meal at the Swan inn; the waiter brought him the wrong dish. Scarcely had Beethoven spoken a few words about the matter, which the waiter answered in a manner not altogether modest, when Beethoven seized the dish (it was a mess of lungs with plenty of gravy) and threw it at the waiter's head. The poor fellow had an armful of other dishes (an adeptness which Viennese waiters possess in a high degree) and could not help himself; the gravy ran down his face. He and Beethoven screamed and vituperated while all the other guests roared with laughter. Finally, Beethoven himself was overcome with the comicalness of the situation, as the waiter who wanted to scold could not, because he was kept busy licking from his chops the gravy that ran down his face, making the most ridiculous grimaces the while. It was a picture worthy of Hogarth.

During his first years in Vienna the composer had enjoyed wearing well-tailored clothes and keeping up certain appearances. After his return from Heiligenstadt, however, he so thoroughly retreated into his music that his rooms became a chaotic mess, which his constant hiring and firing of servants did nothing to improve. Walking about with

Napoleon's troops entered Vienna on November 13, 1805. The French army's progress was so swift that the Austrians put up no serious resistance.

yellow cotton in his ears, he often lost track of day and night, caring for nothing but his music until hunger or fatigue reminded him of more prosaic realities. Nothing better illustrates Beethoven's total obliviousness to the outside world than do his letters and the written recollections of his friends. Except for his rage (described by Ries) when Napoleon assumed the imperial crown, Beethoven rarely registered his reaction to the contemporary turmoil in Europe.

And turmoil there was. In the early years of the nineteenth century Napoleon was closing in on Austria and Germany for the second time. During the autumn of 1805 a siege of Vienna was averted when the city magistrates negotiated a conditional capitulation: Vienna would submit to the French if the safety of its buildings and the lives and property of its citizens were guaranteed. On November 13, 1805, the French army, with Napoleon following on horseback, entered the city. Although he established his official quarters at Schönbrunn, an Austrian imperial palace outside town, the Viennese came to expect his appearance every day.

Napoleon felt somewhat ill at ease in Vienna and did his best to restore the city's busy, artistic atmosphere—while regularly reminding its residents of his presence. He organized frequent parades and reviewed his troops daily. He attended the ballet and opera, encouraged the theater to go on as before, and made certain that his officers filled the concert halls and theaters. But Viennese society largely avoided the performances as a rebuke to Napoleon and the foreign army that occupied their beloved city.

The atmosphere, therefore, was strained on November 20, when *Fidelio*, Beethoven's only opera, first was performed. The subject of the libretto was the power of the spirit of liberty to overcome tyranny. It was based on a story by a Frenchman, Jean-Nicholas Bouilly, who was an administrator in France during the Revolution. Thus, in a way, *Fidelio* (which originally was called *Leonore*, after the heroine) celebrated the ideals of the French Revolution.

It would seem, then, that the audience would have particularly appreciated Beethoven's opera. But this was not the case. For one thing, Napoleon's officers were largely indifferent to music. For another, the obvious shortage of Viennese in the audience at the Theater an der Wien emphasized the paradox: here sat the inheritors of the tradition of the Revolution—and it was they who were the oppressors. Here were the supposed protectors of the rights of

95

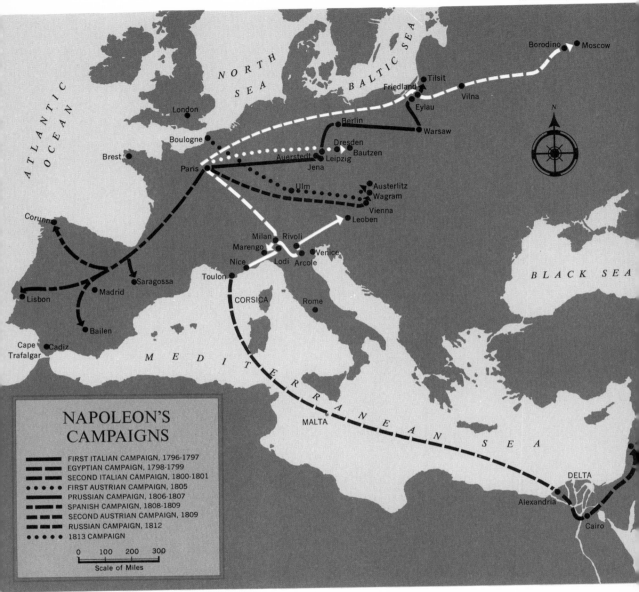

FRANCIS & SHAW, INC.

NORTH SEA

BALTIC SEA

ATLANTIC OCEAN

London

Boulogne

Brest

Paris

Berlin

Dresden

Bautzen

Auerstedt

Leipzig

Jena

Tilsit

Friedland

Eylau

Vilna

Warsaw

Borodino

Moscow

N

Ulm

Austerlitz

Wagram

Vienna

Leoben

Milan

Rivoli

Marengo

Nice

Lodi

Arcole

Venice

Corunna

Madrid

Saragossa

Lisbon

Bailen

Cape Trafalgar

Cadiz

Toulon

CORSICA

Rome

MEDITERRANEAN SEA

BLACK SEA

MALTA

DELTA

Alexandria

Cairo

NAPOLEON'S CAMPAIGNS

—————— FIRST ITALIAN CAMPAIGN, 1796-1797
—— —— —— EGYPTIAN CAMPAIGN, 1798-1799
— — — — SECOND ITALIAN CAMPAIGN, 1800-1801
• • • • • • FIRST AUSTRIAN CAMPAIGN, 1805
—·—·—·— PRUSSIAN CAMPAIGN, 1806-1807
– – – – SPANISH CAMPAIGN, 1808-1809
—— —— —— SECOND AUSTRIAN CAMPAIGN, 1809
■ ■ ■ ■ RUSSIAN CAMPAIGN, 1812
• • • • • 1813 CAMPAIGN

0   100   200   300
Scale of Miles

Marching behind standards depicting the imperial eagle, like the one opposite, the Napoleonic armies occupied Vienna in 1805 and again in 1809. The routes they took are marked respectively by the black dots and short dashes.

man—watching a musical play about violations of the rights of man while they themselves were fulfilling the role of invaders.

The irony was lost on the French officers. For them the main attraction was Beethoven, not his music. He conducted the opera himself, despite his poor hearing, and his lion's mane of black hair flew in every direction as he led the performers with all his energy. *Fidelio*, moreover, was a difficult work: in this first version the singers had not yet mastered many of the parts, and the orchestra was not so well rehearsed as it might have been. The performance was not the great success that the composer would have wished.

For nine years Beethoven struggled to improve *Fidelio*. He always regarded it—probably because of its subject matter—as his noblest work. (According to one friend, Beethoven remarked on his deathbed that, of all his compositions, *Fidelio* was the one most worthy of being studied and emulated by future generations.)

As he was possessed by *Fidelio*, so, too, was he possessed by his devotion to its theme and by Napoleon's failure to remain true to the ideals of the theme. Speaking of Napoleon, he reportedly once said to a fellow musician: "It's a pity that I do not understand the art of war as well as I do the art of music, I would conquer him!"

SCOTTISH UNITED SERVICES MUSEUM, EDINBURGH CASTLE

VI THE MIDDLE YEARS

To this day critics and admirers of Beethoven's music are divided on the issue of *Fidelio*. Some believe it to be the master's noblest, if not his best work. Others think that it fails to justify the long hours and many years that Beethoven spent working on it. But almost all of them agree on one thing: *Fidelio* reveals much about the mind of the composer. It reflects his attitudes about liberty, about love, about good and evil.

Why the librettist, Joseph von Sonnleithner (who adapted the story by Jean Nicolas Bouilly), chose to set the scene in Spain is uncertain. Most likely he did so to avoid the Austrian censors. All literature was closely read and often censored in the Hapsburg principalities; and since *Fidelio* dealt with the theme of individual freedom, Sonnleithner may have decided to transpose the story to a foreign country in order to blur its political significance for contemporary Austria.

Originally *Fidelio* was entitled *Leonore, or Married Love.* Leonore is the heroine and the devoted wife of Florestan. Beethoven was very sentimental about women, and Leonore's selfless dedication to her husband must have appealed to the composer as a worthy second theme to a story about freedom.

As the curtain rises, Florestan is in prison. Apparently his only crime was to attract the hatred of the prison Governor, Don Pizarro, a wicked tyrant. Outside the prison a rumor is spread that Florestan is dead. Leonore refuses to believe it and decides to investigate for herself. She further declares that if Florestan is alive, she will rescue him.

To gain entrance to the prison, Leonore disguises herself as a boy and calls herself Fidelio. (The very name that she

Working from a plaster cast of Beethoven's face, the sculptor Franz Klein created this bronze bust in 1812, when the master was forty-two and perhaps at the height of his fame as one of Europe's foremost composers.

chooses reflects her fidelity.) As Fidelio, she convinces the chief prison keeper, Rocco, to employ her as his assistant.

Meanwhile, Don Pizarro receives word that his rival and superior, Don Fernando, is coming to inspect the prison. Don Fernando is a government minister and apparently a man of high democratic ideals. This is bad news for the wicked Pizarro, because Florestan, another democrat, has been imprisoned illegally. To release Florestan would be impossible: he would only spread the word of Don Pizarro's treachery. To leave him in his cell also would be impossible: Don Fernando would discover him there and realize that Pizarro was using the prison to confine his political enemies. Pizarro's only course is to kill Florestan.

Don Pizarro attempts to persuade Rocco to commit the murder, but Rocco refuses to take the risk. Don Pizarro persists, and Rocco finally agrees to bury Florestan's body if Don Pizarro kills him.

In Act Two, Rocco and his assistant, Fidelio, enter Florestan's cell and begin to dig a grave. Presently, Don Pizarro appears, knife in hand. As the Governor rushes toward Florestan, Fidelio throws herself between them. Don Pizarro is momentarily stunned, but as he regains his composure and moves to complete his task, Fidelio draws a pistol from her boy's garments. She is about to shoot the

Beethoven wrote only one opera, Fidelio. In Act Two, Fidelio, the heroine, intervenes as the wicked Don Pizarro prepares to murder her husband, Florestan. A moment later, she pulls a pistol from her boy's disguise and holds off Don Pizarro until the arrival of the good Don Fernando.

Governor when the blare of distant trumpets announces the approach of Don Fernando. The good minister arrives and immediately recognizes Florestan as a friend and ally. Informed of Don Pizarro's activities and intentions, Don Fernando places him under arrest. The opera ends with a long series of joyful arias about the triumph of liberty, virtue, love, and the devotion of a good wife.

This—very briefly—is the version of *Fidelio* most familiar today. Originally, at the 1805 performance, the opera was given in three acts. A revised version, pared down to two acts, was staged in 1806. Not until 1814—after further revision and more extensive cutting—was the *Fidelio* most commonly heard today presented in Vienna.

Even the overtures to *Fidelio* illustrate Beethoven's never-ending quest for perfection. He wrote four of them. The 1805 opera opened with the overture known as Leonore No. 2. The 1806 performances began with Leonore No. 3. In 1807 a presentation of *Fidelio* was planned tentatively for Prague, and Beethoven intended to use still another overture. Some historians have suggested that this work was in fact Leonore No. 1, the composer's first effort and a simpler version of Leonore No. 2. (According to one colleague of Beethoven's, listeners at a trial performance of the opera at Prince Lichnowsky's house in 1805 believed the first overture too light for so complex a work; and as a result Beethoven replaced it with the more richly scored No. 2.) The 1814 version, officially renamed *Fidelio*, was preceded by yet another introduction, now known as the Fidelio Overture.

Beethoven's suspicious nature seems to have made him unable to believe that any suggestion could be motivated by a serious concern for the music rather than by jealousy or wickedness. Knowing this, his good friends were faced with a dilemma. After the premier of *Fidelio* in 1805 they realized that they must convince Beethoven to shorten the cumbersome score. They also realized that only a conspiracy would persuade him to do so.

Again the setting was the palace of Prince Lichnowsky; it was December, 1805. The opera already had been performed and had generated little enthusiasm. Beethoven himself was sure that the failure was the fault of the tenor who had sung the part of Florestan. His friends thought the explanation more complex—they were convinced that it had to do principally with the length of the opera. In any event, a new Florestan was hired: Josef August Röckel. It was Röckel who recorded the details of the conspiracy:

It was not until we were on our way to the Prince's palace that Mayer [a bass singer] informed me that we would find Beethoven there among his most intimate friends, and that together with the other opera artists who had taken part in the fiasco of his opera "Leonore" we would once more give a critical performance of the work, in order to convince the Master himself of the necessity of a revision. . . . I shuddered at the thought of having to sing the difficult part of Florestan at first sight, for the composer . . . [was] hard to satisfy [and] given to outbursts of passion. . . . I should have liked best of all to turn back again, and would have done so had not Mayer clung to my arm and literally dragged me along with him. . . .

We were led into a music-room with silken draperies, fitted out with chandeliers lavishly supplied with candles. On its walls rich, splendidly colorful oil paintings by the greatest masters, in broad, glittering golden frames bespoke the lofty artistic instincts as well as the wealth of the princely family owning them. . . . The Princess, an elderly lady of winning amiability and indescribable gentleness, yet as a result of great physical suffering . . . pale and fragile, already was sitting at the piano. Opposite her, carelessly

Some years after this portrait was painted, Prince Karl Lichnowsky's wife, Maria Christiane, beseeched Beethoven to make cuts in Fidelio.

As this contemporary sketch shows, Beethoven's hands were broad and powerful—the very antithesis of the long-fingered delicacy traditionally associated with virtuosos.

reclining in an armchair, the fat Pandora-score of his unfortunate opera across his knees, sat Beethoven. . . . After I had been presented to the Prince and Princess, and Beethoven had acknowledged our respectful greetings, he placed his score on the music-desk for the Princess and—the performance began.

The initial two acts . . . were sung from the first to the last note. Eyes sought the clock, and Beethoven was importuned to drop some of the long-drawn sections of secondary importance. Yet he defended every measure, and did so with such nobility and artistic dignity that I was ready to kneel at his feet. But when he came to the chief point at issue itself, the notable cuts . . . which would make it possible to fuse the two acts into one, he was beside himself, shouted uninterruptedly "Not a note!" and tried to run off with his score. But the Princess laid her hands, folded as though in prayer, on the sacred score entrusted to her, looked up with indescribable mildness at the angry genius and behold—his rage melted at her glance, and he once more resignedly resumed his place. . . .

Midnight had passed before the performance . . . at last came to an end. "And the revision, the curtailments?" the Princess asked the Master with a pleading look.

"Do not insist on them," Beethoven answered somberly, "not a single note must be missing."

"Beethoven," she cried with a deep sigh, "must your great work then continue to be misunderstood and condemned?"

"It is sufficiently rewarded with your approval, your Ladyship," said the Master and his hand trembled slightly as it glided over her own.

Then suddenly it seemed as though a stronger, more potent spirit entered into this delicate woman. Half-kneeling and seizing his knees she cried to him as though inspired: "Beethoven! No— your greatest work, you yourself shall not cease to exist in this way! God who has implanted those tones of purest beauty in your soul forbids it, your mother's spirit, which at this moment pleads and warns you with my voice, forbids it! Beethoven, it must be! Give in! Do so in memory of your mother! Do so for me, who am only your best friend!''

The great man, with his head suggestive of Olympian sublimity, stood for many moments before the worshiper of his Muse, then brushed his long, falling curls from his face, as though an enchanting dream were passing through his soul, and, his glance turned heavenward full of emotion, cried amid sobs: "I will—yes, all—I will do all, for you—for my your—for my mother's sake!'' And so saying he reverently raised the Princess and offered the Prince his hand as though to confirm a vow. Deeply moved we surrounded the little group, for even then we all felt the importance of this supreme moment.

From that time onward not another word was said regarding the opera. All were exhausted, and I am free to confess that I exchanged a look of relief not hard to interpret with Mayer when servants flung open the folding-doors of the dining-room, and the company at last sat down to supper at plentiously covered tables. . . . Beethoven . . . ate noticeably little; while I, tormented by the most ravenous hunger, devoured the first course with a speed bordering on the ludicrous. He smiled as he pointed to my empty plate: "You have swallowed your food like a wolf—what have you eaten?'' "I was so famished,'' I replied, "that to tell the truth, I never noticed what it was I ate.''

After the 1814 performance *Fidelio* gradually began to make its way into the repertory of every opera company in Germany and Austria. To generations of nineteenth-century opera lovers it became the anthem of liberty. To generations of nineteenth-century composers it became the prototype of a new kind of music—a music of the emotions, of the human soul.

The story of *Fidelio*'s composition spans nearly the entire "middle period" of the three into which Beethoven's life has been roughly divided by his biographers. Until 1800 his works showed their debt to his predecessors, particularly Haydn and Mozart. In the middle period he developed a recognized and appreciated style of his own. Then, from about 1815 until his death, he composed more complex and introspective works, which frequently puzzled his contemporaries and did not really come into favor until the twentieth century; today they are regarded as his greatest works.

It was the middle period of *Fidelio*, symphonies three through eight, the violin concerto, the third, fourth, and fifth piano concertos, five string quartets, and more than a dozen piano sonatas that made the Romantics claim him as

OVERLEAF: *The "old" Burgtheater of Vienna, as it appears in this colored engraving, became the national theater in 1776. Little more than a century later, it was replaced by the "new" Burgtheater.*

their ancestor. They were particularly fond of music that told a story, attempted to imitate nonmusical sounds (such as birdcalls), or painted musical pictures (of a summer day, a thunderstorm). Beethoven by no means invented "program music," as it is called, and he did not hold it in the highest esteem, but he did write it from time to time.

In a sense, the *Eroica* was Beethoven's first programmed symphony, although only the second movement—the Funeral March—bears a title. By contrast, the sixth, or Pastoral, symphony, is programmed from beginning to end. Each movement has a title, such as "Cheerful impressions awakened by arrival in the country" (first movement). But the composer took care to stress that his work expressed his feeling about the title and was not an attempt to paint the scene literally.

The Pastoral, like the fifth symphony, was dedicated to Prince Lobkowitz and to Count (later Prince) Rasoumovsky, who was the Russian ambassador to Vienna and the brother-in-law of Beethoven's faithful patron Prince Lichnowsky. Rasoumovsky lived very grandly in Vienna and was not only an accomplished violinist but also a real connoisseur of Haydn's quartets. The three quartets that he commissioned Beethoven to write were published in 1808, when the composer also was finishing the Pastoral. From that year until 1816 Rasoumovsky employed a quartet, organized by Schuppanzigh. The quartet became the most distinguished in Europe, and during those years, as one chronicler has put it: "Beethoven was, as it were, cock of the walk in the princely establishment; everything that he composed was rehearsed hot from the griddle and performed to the nicety of a hair, according to his ideas, just as he wanted it and not otherwise. . . ."

Despite this generous reception by one of Vienna's most brilliant musical aristocrats, Beethoven almost moved away from the city at the beginning of 1809 to become first *Kapellmeister* to Jerome Bonaparte, one of Napoleon's brothers. The ruler of France had named this callow young man of twenty-three to be King of Westphalia, and Jerome had offered Beethoven a handsome salary to come to the central German town of Cassel and be his music master.

The composer's financial position was uncertain at the time and he was disgusted by what he imagined to be cabals of rival musicians working against him in Vienna. When she heard of the possible move, Beethoven's old and loyal friend the Countess Erdödy urged him to write down the terms on which he would consent to remain in the city. This

Prince Rasoumovsky's vast palace in Vienna was gutted by a six-hour fire in 1814, during the Congress of Vienna. Even with a loan from the Tsar, the wealthy prince could not afford to build another one.

he did very precisely, stipulating a lifelong annuity and other conditions. True to her word, the Countess circulated the document in the proper quarters. At the beginning of March Prince Lobkowitz, Archduke Rudolph, and a Prince Ferdinand Kinsky signed a long document promising Beethoven everything he had asked and guaranteeing that each would contribute a share of the annuity.

It was a generous gesture by three young men (Rudolph and Kinsky were in their twenties; Lobkowitz only thirty-five), but it did not solve Beethoven's financial problems for

long. Kinsky died after falling from his horse in 1812. A year before, Lobkowitz had gone bankrupt. Only Rudolph consistently kept up his payments, even increasing them to compensate for a devaluation of the Austrian currency in later years. It was entirely characteristic of Rudolph, who remained a devoted student and patron of the composer until Beethoven's death. He was always the model of patience when the master grew angry and when, as happened all too frequently, Beethoven simply failed to turn up at the appointed hour for the imperial music lessons.

In the spring of 1809 Austria took up arms against Napoleon. But within a month the tide of war clearly was running against the Austrians, and the aristocracy began to flee Vienna en masse. Rudolph and the rest of the imperial family left on May 4, only days ahead of the advancing French army. When the city refused to surrender, the French began to bombard it on May 11. Beethoven's quarters were lined up uncomfortably well with the French guns, and he took refuge in the cellar of his brother Carl's house, burying his head under pillows to protect what was left of his hearing from the exploding shells.

The enemy entered the city the next afternoon and exacted reparations in cash and supplies, which caused the cost of living to soar. Even Beethoven, whose new annuity left him comparatively well off, felt the pinch. To make matters worse, the composer could not make his customary summer pilgrimage to the country, for even the suburbs of Vienna were off limits until July. It was a frustrating climax to a decade of intense creative activity, perhaps unrivaled in terms of quality by any composer at any time.

Beethoven's relatively small output in 1810 may have been caused by his preoccupation with the talented and charming Thérèse Malfatti. He had met her cultivated, musical family several years before in Vienna, but his passion for Thérèse did not develop until the summer of 1810, which the composer and the Malfattis spent in Teplitz.

During the brief affair the composer behaved most uncharacteristically. He was so delighted when the Malfattis' dog, Gigons, followed him home that he wrote about it to a friend (one of two surviving notices that he was aware of the existence of domestic animals). He even began to worry

Years afterward, Beethoven recalled that he had written the "Scene by the Brook" for the Pastoral Symphony near Nussdorf, "and the yellowhammers . . . the quails, nightingales and cuckoos . . . composed with me."

OVERLEAF: *While Napoleon bombarded Vienna on the night of May 11, 1809, Beethoven took shelter in his brother Carl's cellar.*

111

about his appearance. He wrote to one friend in Vienna asking for linen for shirts and "at least half a dozen neckties" and to another requesting a mirror. He ends the second letter with pathetic sincerity: "Farewell and don't write again about me as a great man—for I have never felt the strength of human nature as I feel it just now." Then he wrote Wegeler asking him to trace his baptismal certificate, which he would have to produce in order to marry.

Three months later it was all over. Thérèse had turned him down. He was thirty-nine and nearly deaf; she was eighteen and heard the voice of the world very clearly.

Of his many summer stopping places, Beethoven must have remembered Teplitz particularly vividly, for it was there, too, that he composed the three passionate letters to an unidentified woman whom he called his "immortal beloved." They bear the day and the month—"July 6, in the morning," "Evening, Monday, July 6," and "Good morning, on July 7," but they do not tell the year. In light of the most recent research, it seems certain that they were written during the summer of 1812 at Teplitz. However, there is

WIEMAR

When they met at Teplitz in 1812, Beethoven, right, and Goethe, left, were renowned all over Europe: the former for his powerful music, the latter for his magnificent poetry.

BEETHOVEN-HAUS, BONN

114

no evidence that they ever were mailed, for they were found after Beethoven's death in a secret compartment in his desk. There also is no positive identification of the lady to whom they were addressed, although Josephine von Brunsvik remains among the strongest contenders. Their teacher-student relationship had ripened into a deeply emotional one from 1805 to 1807. Now, in late May or early June, 1812, Josephine became estranged from her second husband. Nonetheless, she gave birth to a daughter ten months later. Was Beethoven perhaps the father, and was Josephine therefore his "immortal beloved"? We probably shall never know.

Though still in bed [begins the third letter], my thoughts go out to you, my Immortal Beloved, now and then joyfully, then sadly, waiting to learn whether or not fate will hear us—I can live only wholly with you or not at all—Yes, I am resolved to wander so long away from you until I can fly to your arms and say that I am really at home with you, and can send my soul enwrapped in you into the land of spirits. . . . No one else can ever possess my heart —never—never—Oh God, why must one be parted from one whom one so loves. . . . Be calm—love me—today—yesterday— what tearful longings for you—you—you—my life—my all— farewell.—Oh continue to love me—never misjudge the most faithful heart of your beloved.

ever thine
ever mine   L.
ever ours.

Josephine von Brunsvik, portrayed here in a miniature on ivory, may have been the lady Beethoven was thinking of when he wrote the three letters (which he never mailed) to an unnamed "immortal beloved."

In all three letters he addresses the unknown lady as "du," which in German is the intimate way of saying "you." In all his surviving correspondence this is the only time the composer addressed a lady as "du." If that were not enough, the very incoherence of these letters would testify to the passionate sincerity of the writer. Beethoven at the age of forty-two was in love the way many men half his age are in love—frantically and without reservations.

Not three weeks after writing to the "immortal beloved," and while he was still at Teplitz, the composer first met Goethe, Germany's greatest poet. They had known each other by reputation and through the charming but unreliable letters of their mutual friend Bettina Brentano. Ironically, Bettina was not present at the several meetings of the two men she most admired in the world. They appraised each other respectfully and shrewdly, but neither found the other quite so perfect as Bettina's letters would have led him to believe. Goethe wrote of the composer: "His talent amazed me; unfortunately he is an utterly un-

OVERLEAF: Several performances of Beethoven's music were given in the ballroom of the Hofburg, a rambling and impressive complex of buildings that was the Viennese home of the rulers of Austria.

115

tamed personality, who is not altogether in the wrong in holding the world to be detestable but surely does not make it any the more enjoyable either for himself or others by his attitude. He is easily excused, on the other hand, and much to be pitied, as his hearing is leaving him, which, perhaps mars the musical part of his nature less than the social. He is of a laconic nature and will become doubly so because of this lack." And Beethoven, who so admired Goethe's writing that he set a number of his poems to music, said: "Goethe is too fond of the atmosphere of the Courts, more so than is becoming to a poet. Why laugh at the absurdities of virtuosi when poets who ought to be the first teachers of a nation, forget all else for the sake of this glitter?"

In the autumn the composer went from Teplitz to Linz, where his brother Johann was working as a druggist. Being a bachelor, Johann had rented part of his house to a doctor and his wife. Then Thérèse Obermeyer, the doctor's sister-in-law, had come to join them, and in the course of time she had become Johann's housekeeper and finally his mistress. It was to break off this liaison that Beethoven traveled to Linz. He appealed to the bishop and to the civil authorities and at last obtained an official order to the effect that the police would remove Thérèse bodily and send her to Vienna if she had not left Johann's house voluntarily by a certain date. Johann and Ludwig had a violent argument, and the dispute was settled only when, on November 8, Johann married Thérèse.

At the same time that he was meddling so vigorously in his brother's private life, Beethoven was able to complete his eighth symphony—an excellent example of how the composer often managed to exist on two levels at once. One of the local newspapers announced his arrival in Linz triumphantly and called him "the Orpheus and great musical poet of our time," and the citizens, as usual, made the best of his eccentricities. During one musical evening at the house of a Count von Dönhoff, Beethoven refused to improvise before dinner. But when the guests had trooped into the dining room, he could not be found. As soon as they all had sat down, he began to play in the drawing room, and one by one, they left the table and gathered around him. After an hour he remembered that he had been called to dinner and hurried off toward the dining

Archduke Rudolf of Austria, Beethoven's mild and infinitely patient pupil and patron, appears in his robes as Cardinal and Archbishop of Olmütz.

The title page of Beethoven's Battle Symphony, above, shows the Duke of Wellington riding to victory at Vittoria. The mediocre symphony was widely acclaimed.

room. On the way, he blundered into a table stacked with dishes and sent them all crashing to the floor. The Count laughed off that loss and accepted with good grace the partial ruination of his pianoforte, for when Beethoven had finished his impromptu concert, half the strings were broken.

No sooner had Beethoven turned one brother's life upside down than he had to help the other. During the winter of 1813 Carl fell gravely ill of consumption and Ludwig lent him money, although he really could not afford to do so. At this time only the ever-faithful Archduke Rudolph was keeping up the annuity payments agreed on in 1809.

This preoccupation with money perhaps explains the composer's willing collaboration with Johann Mälzel, the inventor of the metronome and—among other mechanical marvels—the Panharmonicon, a sort of music box that reproduced the sounds of a military band.

Mälzel planned to take his music box to England later in the year and play the pieces by Haydn, Handel, and Cherubini that already were transcribed onto cylinders made for the machine. Shrewdly, he anticipated a greater success for the English trip if he could announce the inclusion of a new piece by Beethoven written expressly for the Panharmonicon. The composer always had admired the British (without ever visiting England), and he readily agreed to collaborate with Mälzel.

During the summer the inventor sketched out a symphony to celebrate the Duke of Wellington's victory at Vittoria, which had taken place that June. Beethoven filled in the outline and included snatches of "Rule Britannia" and "God Save the King." Then, when the English trip began to look uncertain, Beethoven scored the Battle Symphony for full orchestra, again on Mälzel's suggestion. Mälzel then arranged its *première* at a large public concert in Vienna that December. The concert was such a success that it was repeated four days later and again early in January.

There is every indication that Beethoven wrote the Battle Symphony because he needed money, and that musically speaking, he always considered it a huge joke. The irony is that it enormously increased his popularity and contributed to the revival of *Fidelio* in the summer of 1814.*

As one of his chroniclers has put it: "The end of the second period [in Beethoven's life] showed us the composer on a plane of celebrity which may fairly be described as one of the loftiest ever reached by a musician in the course of his artistic strivings." And when the rulers of Europe converged on Vienna for the great Congress that officially ended the tyranny of Napoleon, Beethoven met them all at Rasoumovsky's and Archduke Rudolph's. The chronicler continues: "It was not without emotion that the great master recalled those days in the Imperial castle and the palace of the Russian Prince and once he told with a certain pride how he had suffered the crowned heads to pay court to him and had always borne himself with an air of distinction."

*Beethoven unjustly refused to pay Mälzel any of the proceeds of the Battle Symphony. When Mälzel managed to assemble a score and present the symphony in Munich, Beethoven was furious and sued him.

VII THE MASTER

The last decade of Beethoven's life illustrates best of all his remarkable ability to exist on two levels. Musically, it was the period of the last piano sonatas, the *Missa Solemnis*, the extraordinary ninth symphony, and his five last, intense quartets. Although his contemporaries were often perplexed by the introspective style of the "late" Beethoven, most modern critics agree that these are not only the composer's most original creations, but also some of the most sublime music ever written.

On the other hand, it was a decade of increasing disorder in his personal habits and in his household and of a growing vindictiveness that was less disastrous for the servants—who could (and did) walk out—than for the members of his own family who could not. In particular, it was a decade marked by an agonizing custody fight for his nephew Karl and a deeply emotional and mutually destructive relationship with the boy.

In 1815 the composer's brother Carl died of consumption. In his will he asked that his widow, Johanna, and Ludwig be made joint guardians of his nine-year-old son, Karl. And in the will he made a special plea that the two guardians forget their past differences.

Predictably, Beethoven did nothing of the kind. As soon as Carl was dead, he informed the police that his brother had been poisoned. During the inquest Beethoven took care of young Karl, forbidding him to see his mother. When the poisoning charge was proved groundless, Beethoven filed suit, claiming that Johanna was an unfit mother and that he should be the child's sole legal guardian.

The composer based his claim on a single instance of infidelity that Johanna had been guilty of early in her mar-

Beethoven became increasingly cantankerous in his later years. He allowed Ferdinand Waldmüller, the painter of this portrait, only a single sitting when the picture was commissioned by one of his music publishers in 1823.

Frau Nanette Streicher was kinder than this water color would indicate. For more than a decade before his death, she helped Beethoven keep his house in order.

riage to Carl. There is no evidence that she was ever again unfaithful, but Beethoven used the one proven instance as a precedent for all sorts of charges. No calumny was too preposterous, and because he was the great Beethoven, his allegations carried some weight.

Beethoven's intentions were not entirely evil, but simply unrealistic. He once wrote to the court: ". . . I feel myself better fitted than anybody else to *incite my nephew to virtue and industry by my own example*." The courts agreed, up to a point. In 1816 the Upper Austrian *Landrecht* awarded Beethoven sole custody of Karl.

But Beethoven was a poor guardian. He neglected Karl and yet expected him to live up to standards for which he had had no preparation. After having won custody, Beethoven immediately enrolled Karl in a fashionable boarding school. After two years Beethoven withdrew the boy and engaged a private tutor for him.

Now Beethoven appealed to his old friend Frau Nanette Streicher, the daughter of a famous piano manufacturer named Stein, to help him put his house in sufficient order to make it an acceptable home for the boy. She had tidied up before and did so again, particularly in the matter of servants. Patiently she answered his questions about how often they ought to be allowed roast meat and how much wine and beer they should have.

When Karl moved in with him, Beethoven expected him to become a great musician, regardless of the fact that he had no talent. The boy reacted to his stern task master by escaping the house as often as possible and several times ran away to his mother. On one occasion Beethoven sent the police to fetch him. As Karl later admitted: "I have become worse because my uncle insisted on making me better."

Responding to Johanna's bribes, the servants occasionally would help Karl secretly to visit his mother, whom he missed terribly and whom Beethoven would not allow him to see. When the master was at his most temperamental, Karl learned that he could improve his uncle's frame of mind by downgrading Johanna.

Meanwhile, in 1818, the matter of Karl's custody came before the courts again. At a hearing it was established that Beethoven was not of noble birth and that therefore a lower court, not the *Landrecht*, should have been handling the case. Beethoven's humiliation was compounded when the lower court gave Karl back to Johanna. Beethoven persisted, however, and possibly by using his influence, had the lower

court decision reversed. Once again he was granted the exclusive custody of his young nephew.

Beethoven knew scarcely anything about children. When Karl behaved, the master would caress him; when he disobeyed, he would beat him. Moreover, Karl never could be certain what behavior his uncle might consider agreeable or disagreeable from one day to the next. Karl was a spirited but average youth who liked to play billiards and wanted to be a soldier. In order to live tolerably with Beethoven, he had to become a chronic liar. The relationship, in short, was a troubling and emotionally costly one to both uncle and nephew.

Only one of the master's close friends—Stephan von Breuning—had the courage to attempt to intervene. In 1817 Breuning advised Beethoven against adopting the boy. Beethoven grew extremely angry and denounced his friend to others (who probably agreed with Breuning). He refused, for many years, to renew his friendship with Breuning.

Yet during these troubled years Beethoven was working on the *Missa Solemnis* ("Solemn Mass"), the second of his

Beethoven, among others, played in the concert hall, above, of the Streicher pianoforte company in Vienna. The composer often suggested improvements in the instruments to the owner, Andreas Streicher, the husband of Nanette.

125

For nearly fifteen years after Beethoven's death his friend Anton Schindler, right, labored on a biography that became a primary source for all subsequent books about the composer and his work.

two masses and a remarkable choral work. Anton Schindler, a violinist and conductor, and the composer's unofficial secretary on and off from 1814 until his death, has left this account of a moment in the year 1819:

Toward the end of August, accompanied by the musician Johann Horzalka, . . . I arrived at the master's home in Mödling. It was four o'clock in the afternoon. As soon as we entered we learned that in the morning both servants had gone away, and that there had been a quarrel after midnight which had disturbed all the neighbors, because as a consequence of a long vigil both had gone to sleep and the food which had been prepared had become unpalatable. In the living-room, behind a locked door, we heard the master singing parts of the fugue in the *Credo*—singing, howling, stamping. After we had been listening a long time to this almost awful scene, and were about to go away, the door opened and Beethoven stood before us with distorted features, calculated to excite fear. He looked as if had been in mortal combat with the whole host of contrapuntists, his everlasting enemies. His first utterances were confused, as if he had been disagreeably surprised at our having overheard him. Then he reached the day's happenings and with obvious restraint he remarked: "Pretty doings, these, everybody has run away and I haven't had anything to eat since yesternoon!" I tried to calm him and helped him to make his toilet. My companion hurried on in advance to the restaurant . . . to have something made ready for the famished master. Then he complained about the wretched state of his domestic affairs. . . . Never, it may be said, did so great an artwork as is the *Missa Solemnis* see its creation under more adverse circumstances.

In 1820 Johanna van Beethoven appealed to the Emperor to return her son to her. The Emperor refused, and the court cases came to an end. Although tragedy was ahead, the matter seemed closed: Karl, whom Beethoven began to refer to as "son," remained with him almost until Beethoven's death.

Beethoven did love Karl, but it appears that he occasionally was conscience-stricken about the boy's mother. Since becoming totally deaf, he had taken to keeping "conversation" books in which others conversed with him and he sometimes conversed with himself. An 1818 entry mentions the litigation between himself and Johanna (whom he refers to only as "the widow"):

For many years after Stephan von Breuning, above, gave Beethoven his frank advice about adopting Karl, the two friends did not speak. The breach was healed only during the composer's last days.

I have done my part, O Lord! It might have been possible without offending the widow, but it was not. Only thou, Almighty God, canst see into my heart, knowest that I have sacrificed my very best for the sake of my dear Karl: bless my work, bless the widow! Why cannot I obey all the prompting of my heart and help the widow?

God, God! my refuge, my rock, O my all! Thou seest my inmost thoughts, thou knowest how it hurts me to be compelled to make others suffer in my good works for my deal Karl!!! O hear me, Ineffable One, hear me, thy unhappy, unhappiest of all mortals!

Beethoven's last years were clouded by other worries besides the long conflict with Karl and Johanna. Many of his friends had died or disappeared; some had been ruined or expelled, Breuning-fashion, from the master's inner circle. The composer no longer attempted to conceal his deafness, but he refused to admit that it limited him. In 1822 he insisted on conducting a rehearsal of *Fidelio*, until orchestra and singers were in a state of total confusion. No one dared tell him; none of the performers had the courage to stop, and he alone in the concert hall was unaware of the chaos. Finally Schindler passed him a note: "Please do not go on; more at home." Beethoven at once understood what had happened. Humiliated, he immediately left the hall and

In Mödling, only nine miles from the center of Vienna, Beethoven worked on his Missa Solemnis *and his grandiose ninth symphony.*

ran home. Later, Schindler found him deeply depressed.

The critic Friedrich Rochlitz met Beethoven during his last years:

Picture to yourself a man of approximately fifty years of age, small rather than of medium size, but with a very powerful, stumpy figure, compact and with a notably strong bone structure . . . a red, healthy complexion; restless, glowing, and when his gaze is fixed even piercing eyes . . . in his whole attitude that tension, that uneasy, worried striving to hear peculiar to the deaf who are keenly sensitive . . .

In broken sentences he made some friendly and amiable re-
marks to me. I raised my voice as much as I could, spoke slowly,
with sharp accentuation. . . . He stood close beside me, now
gazing on my face with strained attention, now dropping his
head. Then he would smile to himself, nod amiably on occasion,
all without saying a word. Had he understood me? Had he failed
to understand? At last I had to make an end, and he gave my
hand a powerful grip and said curtly to [Tobias Haslinger, a
music publisher]: "I still have a few necessary errands to do."
Then, as he left, he said: "Shall we not see each other again?"
[Haslinger] now returned. "Did he understand what I said?" I

queried. I was deeply moved and affected. [Haslinger] shrugged his shoulders. "Not a word!" For a long time we were silent and I cannot say how affected I was . . . The man who solaced the whole world with the voice of his music, heard no other human voice, not even that of one who wished to thank him. Aye, it even became an instrument of torture for him.

In 1824 Beethoven was ready to present his *Missa Solemnis* and his ninth symphony to the public. But he decided that the Viennese no longer understood or appreciated his works and he tried to arrange a *première* of the two masterpieces in Berlin. A group of distinguished Viennese nobles, including Count Moritz Lichnowsky, brother of the composer's patron Karl, and the music publisher Steiner signed a petition imploring Beethoven to present the works in Vienna. Moved by this expression of admiration, Beethoven consented to do so.

The performance took place at the Court Theater on May 7. The master conducted, although the orchestra and chorus more closely followed the direction of the assistant conductor, Michael Umlauf, who stood behind and below Beethoven. The applause at the end was tumultuous—although Beethoven could not hear it. He stood with his back to the audience until one of the singers, Fraulein Unger, turned him around. Knowing that he was deaf, the audience stamped and shouted, hoping to show him his triumph. Although he could not have failed to appreciate the ovation, the master remembered the concert mainly as a terrific disappointment: because of the production expenses, the profits from it were much smaller than he had hoped they would be.

Characteristically, Beethoven suspected that his friends had somehow cheated him out of some of the profits. As though to celebrate the artistic triumph, he invited Schindler, Umlauf, and Schuppanzigh to dinner. Then an angry Beethoven unfairly accused his three loyal friends of double dealing.

Yet before long the composer would face problems that were real enough. In July, 1826, his nephew Karl bought a pistol and attempted to commit suicide. He succeeded only in wounding himself superficially in the head and was hospitalized.

Beethoven begged Karl to tell him the reason for his despair, but Karl could not answer and turned his face to the wall. Beethoven himself then fell ill, and he and Karl went to the composer's brother Johann's four-hundred-acre estate at Gneixendorf near Vienna in order to convalesce.

In the "conversation" book above, Beethoven writes in French and Schindler replies in German. The ear trumpets, below, were designed and made by Mälzel when the inventor and the composer collaborated on the Battle Symphony.

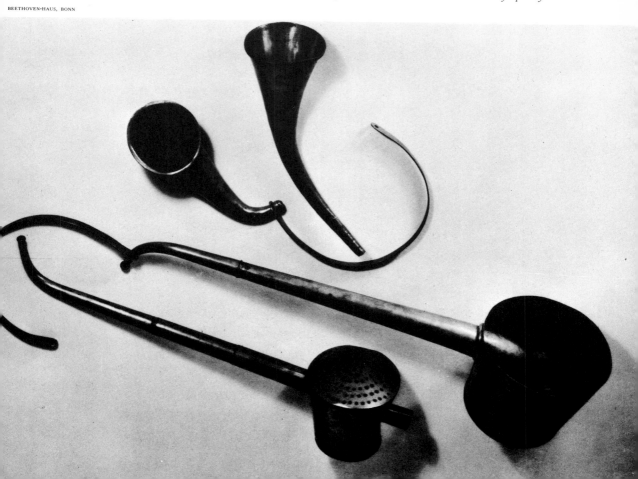

There the master tried to get Johann to make a will favoring Karl rather than his own wife. Karl implored his uncle to drop the matter. "Why do you make such a disturbance?" he wrote in one of the conversation books. And later in the same conversation the boy's exasperation is clear: "I'll come again later—I only want to go to my room—I am not going out, I want only to be alone for a little while. Will you not let me go to my room?"

Beethoven would wake at five-thirty in the morning, and he would write for two hours until breakfast, at which he would ignore his relatives. With his notebook in hand, he would walk in the fields, stomping and waving his arms and shouting; once he even stampeded a team of young oxen with his shouts. This eccentric method of composing led the local folk to believe that he was mad. At half past noon he would have lunch, go to his room until three o'clock, and then walk again until sundown. Dinner was at seven-thirty. After eating, he would work again until he went to bed at ten.

In December, after a violent quarrel with Johann, Beethoven returned to Vienna with Karl. It was a damp, cold journey, and on his arrival the composer fell ill with pneumonia and began to cough up blood. No sooner had the pneumonia responded to treatment than he contracted dropsy. In all probability he already was suffering from jaundice, and this affliction, too, became worse. His body swelled so grotesquely that his stomach had to be bandaged, and he turned the yellow color symptomatic of the disease. A physician, according to the accepted practice of the day, repeatedly punctured his stomach to draw off the accumulated water. At various times, sweat baths, ice compresses, and frozen punch were prescribed. Beethoven seemed to thrive on the punch and even talked of working on his tenth symphony. But then he drank too much of it and suffered a relapse.

Meanwhile, Karl finally had been allowed to join the army and had left Vienna early in January, never to see his uncle again. Among the composer's small pleasures during his last illness was the gift of the complete scores of Handel, who was among Beethoven's favorite composers. The Philharmonic Society of London, having heard of his state, sent him £100. In March, 1827, a shipment of rare wine arrived. The master, who was very fond of this particular vintage, commented simply, "Pity, pity—too late!"

Stephan von Breuning maintained an apartment in the same house, the Schwarzspanierhaus, a former monastery, and his thirteen-year-old son Gerhard was Beethoven's most frequent visitor. "Has your belly become smaller? . . ." the child would write in the conversation book. "Are you supposed to perspire more? . . . Are you finished with Walter Scott?"

March 26 was a snowy, stormy day. A flash of lightning illuminated the room. Beethoven lifted his hand—some say that he was shaking his fist at heaven—then he stiffened and died. The musician Hüttenbrenner held the master's head and closed the staring eyes. Frau van Beethoven, Johann's abused wife, cut a lock of his hair. It was just before six o'clock in the evening.

Perhaps remembering Mozart's shameful funeral, twenty thousand Viennese joined Beethoven's cortege. The poet Franz Grillparzer wrote the following funeral oration:

Standing by the grave of him who had passed away, we are in a manner the representatives of an entire nation, of the whole German people, mourning the loss of the one highly acclaimed half of that which was left us of the departed splendor of our native art, of the fatherland's full spiritual bloom. . . . the last master of tuneful song, the organ of soulful concord, the heir and amplifier of Handel and Bach's, of Haydn and Mozart's immortal fame is now no more, and we stand weeping over the riven strings of the harp that is hushed.

The young Gerhard von Breuning, above, was Beethoven's neighbor in the Schwarzspanierhaus, below. He won the dying composer's affection with his cheerful prattle.

The harp that is hushed! Let me call him so! For he was an artist, and all that was his, was his through art alone. The thorns of life had wounded him deeply, and as the cast-away clings to the shore, so did he seek refuge in thine arms, . . . heaven-born Art! To thee he clung fast, and even when . . . his deaf ear had blinded his vision for thy features, still did he ever carry thine image within his heart. . . .

He was an artist, but a man as well. A man in every sense—in the highest. Because he withdrew from the world, they called him a man-hater, and because he held aloof from sentimentality, unfeeling . . . He fled the world because, in the whole range of his loving nature, he found no weapon to oppose it. . . . He withdrew from mankind after he had given them his all and received nothing in return. He dwelt alone, because he found no second Self. But to the end his heart beat warm for all men, in fatherly affection for his kindred, for the world his all and his heart's blood.

Thus he was, thus he died, thus he will live to the end of time.

You, however, who have followed after us hitherward, let not your hearts be troubled! You have not lost him, you have won him. No living man enters the halls of the immortals. Not until the body has perished, do their portals unclose. He whom you

This sketch of the dying Beethoven shows how wasted the composer's powerful body became during the four months of his fatal illness.

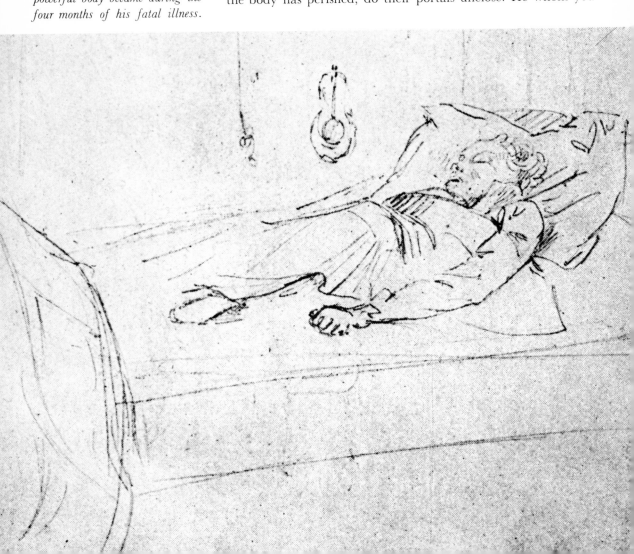

Franz Grillparzer, long the composer's friend, wrote Beethoven's funeral oration. The two men often had discussed the possibility of collaborating on an opera, but nothing had come of the idea. Frequently in trouble with the strict censors of the Hapsburg regime, Grillparzer was not recognized as Austria's greatest dramatic poet until a century after his death.

The sun streams through the window of Beethoven's study in the Schwarz-spanierhaus. The inkstand is ready on the sill, and the piano, littered with papers, as usual, seems to be waiting for the composer. But Beethoven will not stomp in. He died three days before this drawing was made.

The exhausting struggle of wills between Beethoven and Karl, his nephew and ward, ended only with the composer's death and the boy's eager entrance into the army.

mourn stands from now onward among the great of all ages, inviolate forever. Return homeward therefore, in sorrow, yet resigned! And should you ever in times to come feel the overpowering might of his creations like an onrushing storm, when your mounting ecstasy overflows in the midst of a generation yet unborn, then remember this hour, and think, We were there, when they buried him, and when he died, we wept.

Alone, aloof, a madman in the opinion of strangers, Beethoven composed his greatest music in his last years. It was not always understood by his contemporaries. His last quartets, for example, were so complex, so advanced, that not until the twentieth century were they fully appreciated. Similarly, a series of variations for the piano on a theme by the composer Diabelli was thought to be too difficult and too obscure for most nineteenth-century musicians. (In a way the Diabelli Variations may have been physically beyond the capabilities of Beethoven's contemporaries. For

OVERLEAF: *Beethoven was buried on March 29, 1827, a day that Vienna would not soon forget. The schools were closed and the funeral procession attracted such enormous crowds that the composer's relatives and friends had the greatest difficulty squeezing into St. Stephan's Cathedral for the service.*

On the initiative of a committee headed by the composer Franz Liszt, Bonn finally erected a monument to its famous native son, Beethoven. It was unveiled in 1845.

the piano in those days was not nearly the strong, versatile instrument it is now. It was almost as though Beethoven had composed the work for a piano yet to be invented.)

To most people the music of the late period is exemplified in the powerful ninth symphony. The work is a summing-up, a hymn to joy—both figuratively and literally. It commences not with a blast as does the fifth, but richly, quietly, almost ominously. The strings murmur, the tympani pound, the volume quickly increases; a horn enters briefly, then falls silent. Comparing the first movements of the fifth and ninth symphonies, J. W. N. Sullivan writes:

Fate [in the ninth] is no longer personified as some sort of powerful enemy that sufficient courage can defy [as in the fifth]. . . . It is now a truly universal destiny, too complete to evoke any thought of resistance. The brooding mystery from which the theme emerges is, like the primeval darkness that preceded creation, something that conditions the human world, but which is not part of it. . . . As the answer to this fate theme Beethoven gives us no more than submission and resignation.

Left, as Sullivan suggests, "with nothing but utter despair and pain" at the end of the first movement, the composer now reverses his usual order and presents not the traditional slow movement but the rhythmic scherzo. Here, in Sullivan's words, "we have once more that unconquerable uprising of blind energy that was the very core" of Beethoven.

The slow movement is one of Beethoven's most beautiful. It is serene, accepting, understanding. An incredibly beautiful melody recurs, suggesting an inner peace that has overcome the adversities of life. "Superhuman ecstacy," Sullivan called it, worth "whatever price has been paid for it." The symphony might well end here. But it does not.

The fourth movement is the most remarkable and the best known. Shortly after its introduction the orchestra replays the main theme of the first movement. But scarcely has the theme been suggested when it is interrupted—it is as though the orchestra were rejecting it. Then, just as briefly, the theme of the scherzo is reviewed and rejected. The main theme of the slow movement receives the same treatment. Now the themes of the symphony have been summarized and refused. What next?

The orchestra blares and then a voice is heard. "Oh, friends, friends," the singer begins, "not these sounds! Let us sing something more pleasant, more full of gladness. O Joy, let us praise thee."

The movement now becomes a chorale—the words are the "Ode to Joy" by the poet Schiller. Beethoven long had wanted to put these words to music, and his ninth symphony ends with them. Joy—the God-descended daughter of Elysium—becomes the unifier of all mankind. It can be expressed, Beethoven seems to be saying, only with human voices. The words are sung in every possible way—nobly, softly, martially, for joy belongs to everyone.

And joy was Beethoven's musical legacy to the world.

OVERLEAF: *This life mask, made when Beethoven was forty-two years old, is the most authentic rendition we have of his features.*

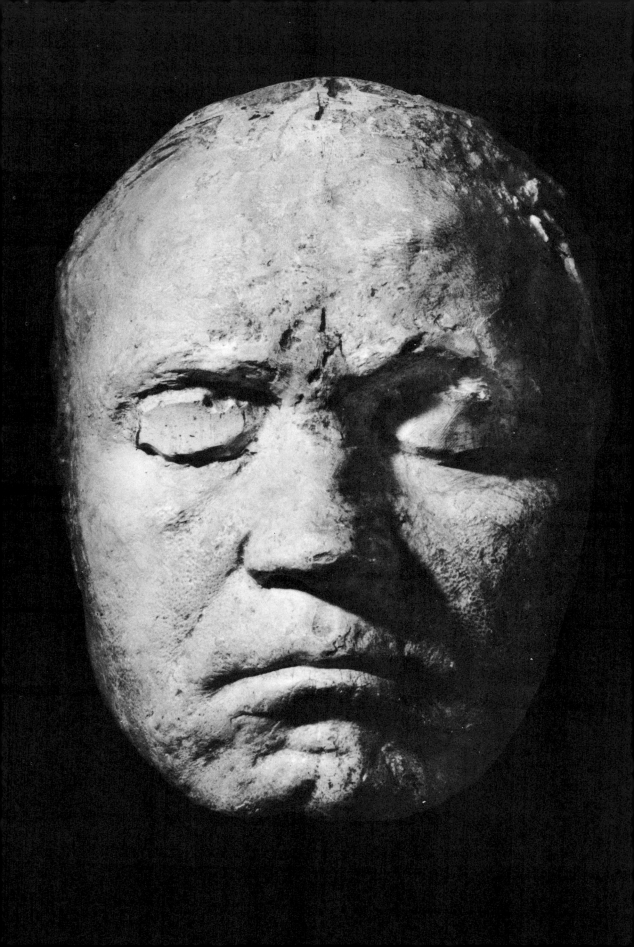

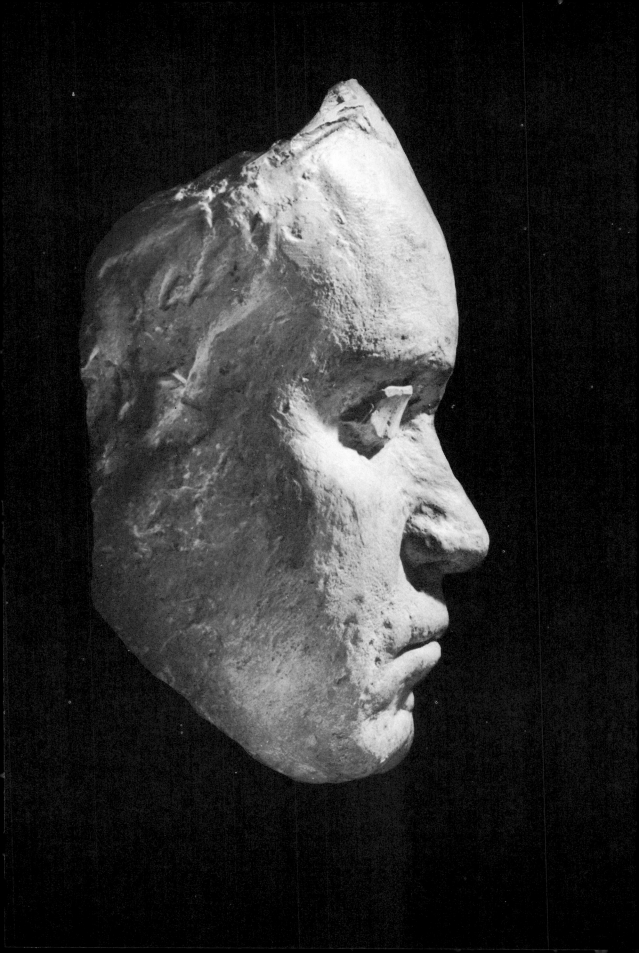

ODE TO JOY

Beethoven adapted these stanzas from Schiller's "Ode to Joy" for the choral movement of his ninth symphony. The translation is by Louis Untermeyer.*

Baritone: O friends, friends, not these sounds!
Let us sing something more pleasant, more
full of gladness. O Joy, let us praise thee!

Joy, thou source of light immortal,
   Daughter of Elysium,
Touched with fire, to the portal
   Of thy radiant shrine we come.
Thy pure magic frees all others
   Held in Custom's rigid rings;
Men throughout the world are brothers
   In the haven of thy wings.

He who knows the pride and pleasure
   Of a friendship firm and strong,
He who has a wife to treasure,
   Let him swell our mighty song.
If there is a single being
   Who can call a heart his own,
And denies it—then, unseeing,
   Let him go and weep alone.

Joy is drunk by all God's creatures
   Straight from earth's abundant breast;
Good and bad, all things are nature's,
   And with blameless joy are blessed.
Joy gives love and wine; her gladness
   Makes the universe her zone,
From the worm that feels spring's madness
   To the angel near God's throne.

Glad, as when the suns run glorious
   Through the deep and dazzling skies,
   Brothers, run with shining eyes—
Heroes, happy and victorious.

Joy, thou source of light immortal,
   Daughter of Elysium,
Touched with fire, to the portal
   Of thy radiant shrine we come.
Thy pure magic frees all others
   Held in Custom's rigid rings;
Men throughout the world are brothers
   In the haven of thy wings.

Millions, myriads, rise and gather!
   Share this universal kiss!
   Brothers, in a heaven of bliss,
Smiles the world's all-loving Father.
Do the millions, His creation,
   Know Him and His works of love?
   Seek Him! In the heights above
Is His starry habitation!

Joy, thou source of light immortal,
   Daughter of Elysium,
Touched with fire, to the portal
   Of thy radiant shrine we come.
Thy pure magic frees all others
   Held in Custom's rigid rings;
Men throughout the world are brothers
   In the haven of thy wings.

Millions, myriads, rise and gather!
   Share this universal kiss!
   Brothers, in a heaven of bliss,
Smiles the world's all-loving Father.
Do the millions, His creation,
   Know Him and His works of love?
   Seek Him! In the heights above.
     Brothers! Brothers!
     In the heights above
Is His starry habitation!

Joy, O daughter of Elysium,
Thy pure magic frees all others
   Held in Custom's rigid rings;
Men throughout the world are brothers
   In the haven of thy wings.

Millions, myriads, rise and gather!
   Share this universal kiss!
   Brothers, in a heaven of bliss,
Smiles the world's all-loving Father.
Do the millions, His creation,
   Know Him and His works of love?
   Seek Him! In the heights above
Is His starry habitation!

BASIC BEETHOVEN RECORD LIBRARY

Beethoven's cello, two violas, and two violins are preserved today in a museum in Bonn, his birthplace.

BEETHOVEN-HAUS, BONN

Theodore Strongin of *The New York Times'* music department has chosen this listing of Beethoven recordings from among the hundreds available.

SYMPHONIES

Complete Symphonies (9): Walter, Columbia Symphony Orchestra. Columbia D7S-610 (seven records).

OVERTURES

To *Prometheus*, Op. 43: Ansermet, Orch. Suisse Romande. London STS-15064.

To *Egmont*, Op. 84: Klemperer, Philharmonia Orchestra. Angel S-3577 (two records).

To *Fidelio* and *Leonore* 1, 2, and 3: Klemperer, Philharmonia Orchestra. Angel S-36209.

CONCERTOS

For Piano

No. 1 in C, Op. 15: Rubinstein, Leinsdorf, Boston Symphony. Victor LSC-3013.

No. 2 in B flat, Op. 19: Serkin, Ormandy, Philadelphia Orchestra. Columbia MS-6839.

No. 3 in C minor, Op. 37: Rubinstein, Leinsdorf, Boston Symphony. Victor LSC-2947.

No. 4 in G, Op. 58: Rubinstein, Leinsdorf, Boston Symphony. Victor LSC-2848.

No. 5 in E flat, Op. 73: Rubinstein, Leinsdorf, Boston Symphony. Victor LSC-2733.

For Other Instruments

Concerto in D for Violin, Op. 61: Oistrakh, Cluytens, Orch. National Fr. Angel S-35780.

Concerto in C for Violin, Cello, Piano, Op. 56: Laredo, Parnas, Serkin, Schneider, Marlboro Festival Orchestra. Columbia MS-6564.

STRING QUARTETS

Complete String Quartets: Opus numbers 18, 59, 74, 95, 127, 130, 131, 132, 135: Budapest String Quartet. Columbia M3S-606 (MS-6074/6); M4S-616 (MS-6185/8); M5S-677 (MS-6383/7) (twelve records).

TRIOS

For Piano

Complete Piano Trios (9): Beaux Arts Trio. Philips WS-4-007 (four records).

For Strings

In D, Op. 8: Heifetz, Primrose, Piatigorsky. Victor LSC-2550.

Op. 9, Trios 1 and 3: Grumiaux Trio. Philips 900226.

MUSIC FOR PIANO ALONE

Sonatas

No. 8 in C minor, Op. 13 ("Pathetique"): Serkin. Columbia MS-6481.

No. 15 in D, Op. 28 ("Pastoral"): Backhaus. London 6247.

No. 17 in D minor, Op. 31, No. 2 ("Tempest"): Backhaus. London 6365.

No. 18 in E flat, Op. 31, No. 3: Backhaus. London 6366.

No. 21 in C, Op. 53 ("Waldstein"): Gieseking. Odyssey 32160314.

No. 26 in E flat, Op. 81a, ("Lebewohl"): Rubinstein. Victor LSC-2654.

No. 30 in E, Op. 109: Backhaus. London 6246.

No. 31 in A flat, Op. 110: Backhaus. London 6535.

Variations

In E flat, Op. 35 ("Eroica"): Brendel. Vox SVBX-5416 (three records).

On a theme by Diabelli, Op. 120: Serkin. Columbia CML-5246.

OTHER CHAMBER MUSIC

Quintet in E flat for Piano and Winds, Op. 16: Vienna Octet. London STS-15053.

Septet in E flat for Strings and Winds, Op. 20: Members of the Vienna Octet. London 6132.

Octet in E flat for Winds, Op. 103: Baron, New York Woodwind Ensemble. Counterpoint/Esoteric 5559.

Complete Sonatas for Violin and Piano (10): Oistrakh, Oborin. Philips PHS-4-990 (four records).

Complete Sonatas for Cello and Piano (5): Casals, Serkin. Odyssey 32360016 (three records).

Complete Chamber Music for Flute: Rampal, Larde, Marion, Hongne, Veyron-Lacroix. Vox SVBX-577 (three records).

Serenade in D for Flute, Violin, Viola, Op. 25: Rampal, Jarry, Collot. Decca 710116.

VOCAL MUSIC

Fidelio, Op. 72: Ludwig, Vickers, Frick, Berry, Klemperer, Philharmonia Orchestra and Chorus (sung in German). Angel S-3625 (three records).

Missa Solemnis in D, Op. 123: Schwarzkopf, Ludwig, Gedda, Zaccaria, Karajan, Philharmonia Orchestra (sung in Latin). Angel S-3595 (two records).

Incidental Music to Goethe's *Egmont*, Op. 84: Nilsson, Klemperer, Philharmonia Orchestra (sung in German). Angel S-3577 (two records).

Fifteen Songs: Fischer-Dieskau (sung in German and Italian). DGG 139197.

INCIDENTAL MUSIC

Music to Kotzebue's *Die Ruinen von Athen* (*The Ruins of Athens*), Op. 113: Beecham, Royal Philharmonic. Angel S-35509.

ACKNOWLEDGMENTS

The Editors are particularly grateful for the valuable assistance of Urszula Slupik in Paris and Audre Proctor in New York. In addition, they would like to thank the following individuals and organizations:

Beethoven-Haus, Bonn—Maria Rochulus
Deinhard & Company, Koblenz
Historisches Museum der Stadt Wien
Dr. Anthony van Hoboken, Ascona
Österreichische Gesellschaft für Musik, Vienna
Österreichische Nationalbibliothek, Vienna—Hofrat
    Dr. Hans Pauer
Rudolf Stepanek, Vienna
Stadtarchiv, Bonn—Dr. Dietrich Horoldt

The quotations on pages 26, 34–35, 36, 60, 84, 93, 115, 126–127, 133–134, and 137 are from *Thayer's Life of Beethoven*, revised and edited by Elliot Forbes, © 1964 by Princeton University Press. The quotations on pages 103–105 and pages 128–130 are from *Beethoven, Impressions by His Contemporaries*, edited by O. G. Sonneck, © 1926, 1954 by G. Schirmer, Inc. Reprinted by permission.

FURTHER READING

Boyden, D. D. *An Introduction to Music*. Faber & Faber, 1959.

Cannon, B. C., Johnson, A. H., and Waite, W. G. *The Art of Music*. New York: Crowell, 1960.

Forbes, E., ed. *Thayer's Life of Beethoven* (2 vols.). Princeton UP: OUP, 1964.

Grove, G. *Dictionary of Music and Musicians*. Macmillan, 1954.

Hamburger, M., ed. *Beethoven: Letters, Journals and Conversations*. Cape, 1966.

Kerst, F., comp. *Beethoven: The Man and the Artist, as Revealed in His Own Words*. Dover: Constable, 1965.

Pryce-Jones, A. *Beethoven*. DuFour, 1948.

Schindler, A. F. *Beethoven as I Knew Him*. Edited by D. W. MacArdle; translated by C. S. Jolly. Faber & Faber, 1966.

Sonneck, O. G., ed. *Beethoven: Impressions by His Contemporaries*. Dover: Constable, 1968.

Sullivan, J. W. N. *Beethoven: His Spiritual Development*. Allen & Unwin, 1964.

Young, P. M. *Beethoven*. Benn, 1966.

Beethoven spent two summers in Teplitz, a spa in western Czechoslovakia.

HISTORISCHES MUSEUM DER STADT WIEN

INDEX

Boldface indicates pages on which maps or illustrations appear

This faithful portrait of Beethoven was done in 1814.

OESTERREICHISCHE NATIONALBIBLIOTHEK, VIENNA